CHALLENGING EARLY LEARNING

What are the goals of Early Years education? A lot of people ask this question and receive answers ranging from keeping children safe; introducing them to the values of society; encouraging a love of language; and giving them experience of socialising, harmonising and behaving appropriately. This book shares the best strategies to help children grow into even more curious, resilient, happy, articulate and thoughtful learners.

Challenging Early Learning takes James Nottingham's tried and tested and acclaimed 'learning to learn' methodology and applies it to teaching three- to seven-year-olds. Each chapter includes:

- Colourful and stimulating learning activities that will help children learn how to learn.

- Practical 'Now Try This' sections that encourage readers to think about current practice and explore new ideas.

- A Review section that focuses on building a broad tool kit of teaching strategies.

Covering a range of key topics such as feedback, dialogue, growth mindset and the Learning Pit, this book is aimed at all pedagogues, teachers, parents and leaders wanting to challenge the way in which we learn and make learning more challenging.

James and Jill Nottingham started an educational company in 1999 to support local nurseries and schools with the development of Philosophy for Children. This evolved into a multimillion-pound social regeneration project to raise the aspirations and abilities of young people in North East England. With the success of this project, early childhood centres across Scandinavia, Australia and New Zealand wanted to get involved in the Nottinghams' award-winning approaches to challenge, dialogue, feedback, questioning and progress. To meet this demand, Jill and James set up companies in Australia, Denmark, Norway, Sweden, the UK and the USA, and now employ 30 educational experts who lead, demonstrate and guide practitioners and parents in the best ways to enhance young children's learning.

CHALLENGING EARLY LEARNING

Helping Young Children Learn How to Learn

James Nottingham and Jill Nottingham

Routledge
Taylor & Francis Group

LONDON AND NEW YORK

Challenging
LEARNING

First published 2019
by Routledge
2 Park Square, Milton Park, Abingdon, Oxon OX14 4RN

and by Routledge
52 Vanderbilt Avenue, New York, NY 10017

Routledge is an imprint of the Taylor & Francis Group, an informa business

British Library Cataloguing-in-Publication Data
A catalogue record for this book is available from the British Library

Library of Congress Cataloging-in-Publication Data
Names: Nottingham, James, author. | Nottingham, Jill, author.
Title: Challenging early learning : helping young children learn how to learn /
    by James Nottingham and Jill Nottingham.
Description: Abingdon, Oxon ; New York, NY : Routledge, 2019.
Identifiers: LCCN 2018060405 | ISBN 9780367027629 (hardback) |
    ISBN 9780367027650 (pbk.) | ISBN 9780429397929 (ebk)
Subjects: LCSH: Early childhood education. | Cognition in children. | Learning, Psychology of.
Classification: LCC LB1139.23 .N67 2019 | DDC 372.21—dc23
LC record available at https://lccn.loc.gov/2018060405

ISBN: 978-0-367-02762-9 (hbk)
ISBN: 978-0-367-02765-0 (pbk)
ISBN: 978-0-429-39792-9 (ebk)

Typeset in Swis
by Apex CoVantage, LLC
Printed and bound by CPI Group (UK) Ltd, Croydon CRO 4YY

Ava, Phoebe, Harry: our children, our world

CONTENTS

Chapter 3: Developing dialogue with young children — 51

Chapter 4: Engaging children's thinking skills — 61

Chapter 5: Listening, thinking and questioning — 73

Chapter 6: Making progress — 83

ACKNOWLEDGEMENTS

The authors would like to thank the following people for their support and suggestions:

Åse Ranfelt

Astrid Holtz Yates

Bosse Larsson

Dan Henderson

Ellspeth Marshall

Gerda Lundberg

Laura Taylor

Lesley Roberts

Lisa Barrett

Marilyn Keenan

Phil Thompson

Rebecca Spencer

Sarah Unwin

Authors can be contacted through www.challengelearning.com.

FIGURES

THE *CHALLENGING LEARNING* STORY

Challenging Learning was the title I used for my first book back in 2010. I chose the title because it brought together two key themes of my work, and it gave a relevant double meaning – challenging the way in which learning takes place *and* showing how to make learning more challenging.

More recently, *Challenging Learning* is the name my co-founder Jill and I have given to a group of organisations set up in seven countries across Europe and Australasia. These educational companies bring together some of the very best teachers and leaders we know. Together, we transform the most up-to-date and impressive research into best pedagogical practices for nurseries, schools and colleges.

This book continues in the same tradition: challenging learning and making learning more challenging. The main difference between this book and the original *Challenging Learning* title is that this one focusses entirely on how to help younger children learn how to learn. There is still the blend of theory and practice that typifies every book with *Challenging Learning* in the title. This one, though, shares ideas relevant for adults working with children aged three to seven years old.

As you read this book, you will notice we have sometimes referred to 'teachers' and 'teaching'. Please do *not* take this to mean the ideas are suitable only for teachers. In fact, the book is aimed at support staff, teachers *and* leaders. We simply use the terms 'teacher' and 'teaching' as shorthand for the position and pedagogy of *all* adults working with children in early childhood and in the first few years of school.

Each chapter includes some 'Now Try This' sections. These encourage you to think about current practice and to share those ideas with your colleagues. Chatting with someone else about what you think works well (and how you know it does), what you would like to change, and, in an ideal world, what you would like your pedagogy to be like will definitely help you to use this book as the reflective journal it is intended to be.

At the end of each chapter is a review. This is focussed on repertoire and judgement. A broad repertoire – or tool kit of teaching strategies, as some authors call it – is crucial to improving pedagogy. Yet repertoire alone is not sufficient; good judgement is also needed. So, whereas the strategies in this book should be sufficient to broaden your repertoire, your good judgement will come from reflections on your own experiences, from trying out the new strategies with your children and from dialogue with your colleagues. Our suggestions for review are there to help you with your reflections.

As a teacher, you are amongst the most powerful influences on children's lives. Back when we were students ourselves, we all knew exactly which member of staff had high expectations and which had low, which had a good sense of humour and which we suspected had not laughed since childhood. It is the same today for our students: your children know what you expect and what your attitude is! It is not the government, the children's parents or the curriculum that sets the culture (though they all have influence). It is *you* who sets the culture, and so it is *your* actions that count significantly in shaping children's expectations, behaviours and values.

With this book, I hope we can inspire you to ever more expert actions.

With best wishes,

James Nottingham

THE LANGUAGE OF LEARNING

The following terms have been used in the following ways in this book:

ASK Model: A model that helps in planning for and talking about learning for young children. It covers **a**ttitudes, **s**kills and **k**nowledge.

Attitudes: A tendency to act or think in a particular way. Attitudes we ought to encourage in young children include curiosity, determination, open-mindedness and so on.

Cognitive conflict: When people have two beliefs that are in conflict with each other. For example, young children might think that they should be friendly to people but also that they should not talk to strangers.

Concept: A general idea that groups things together according to accepted characteristics. Concepts that young children might think about include fairness, play, friends, feelings, emotions and so on.

Construct: Shorthand for Stage 3 of the Learning Challenge in which children construct meaning by connecting, explaining and examining ideas.

Culture: The behaviours and beliefs that characterise a group of people. Used in the context of developing a positive culture for learning.

Dialogue: Dialogue is conversation and inquiry. Dialogue combines the sociability of conversation with the skills of framing questions and constructing answers.

Educere: The root word in Latin from which the word 'education' comes from. It is used in the book as an acronym for seven categories of thinking.

Fixed mindset: From the work of Carol Dweck (2006, 2012, 2015). A mindset is a self-perception or 'self-theory' that people hold about themselves. A fixed mindset refers to a belief that talents are abilities and more or less fixed by genetics.

Generalisation: A statement based on an identified group of common characteristics.

Growth mindset: Also from the work of Carol Dweck (2006, 2012, 2015). A growth mindset refers to a belief that talents and abilities are 'grown' rather than bestowed by birth.

Knowledge: When children know particular facts. It is different from understanding. Understanding is when children can relate, explain and evaluate.

Learning-focus: A learning-focus includes an emphasis on questioning, challenging, striving to get better and on beating personal bests. This is in contrast to a performance-focus that hinges on grades, attainment and beating other people. In other words, a learning-focus is intrinsic whereas a performance-focus is extrinsic.

Learning Intention: What children should know, understand or be able to do by the end of a defined period of time.

Metacognition: Literally, 'thinking about thinking'. Metacognition is an important part of learning. It encourages children to think about *how* they are thinking and acting and to reflect on whether there is a better way they could do things.

Performance-focus: A focus that hinges on grades, attainment and beating other people. This contrasts with a learning focus, which emphasises questioning, challenging and beating personal bests.

Pit: A metaphor to identify the state of confusion persons feel when holding two or more conflicting thoughts or opinions in their mind at the same time.

Preview: Gives children an idea about what they will be learning in advance of the lesson. This allows them to prepare beforehand. The effect can be significantly positive.

Process: The actions that lead to the Learning Intention. Focussing on process is particularly important when teaching children **how** to learn as much as *what* to learn.

Reflection: Giving serious thought or consideration to a thought, idea or response.

Self-regulation: An ability to control impulses, plan strategically and act thoughtfully.

Self-review: When a child gives himself or herself feedback.

Skills: The abilities to carry out those processes necessary for gaining understanding, completing tasks or performing in any given context.

SOLO Taxonomy: The Structure of Observed Learning Outcomes model describes levels of increasing complexity in the understanding of subjects, originally proposed by John Biggs and Kevin Collis.

Success Criteria: Summary of the key steps or ingredients children need to accomplish the Learning Intention. They include the main things to do, include or focus on.

Taxonomy: A classification representing the intended outcomes of the educational process.

Understanding: The mental process of a person who comprehends. It includes an ability to explain cause, effect and significance and to understand patterns and how they relate to one another.

Wobblers and wobbling: User-friendly terms to describe a state of cognitive conflict.

Zone of Proximal Development: Used by Lev Vygotsky to describe the zone between actual and potential development.

1. CREATING THE CONDITIONS FOR EARLY LEARNING

> CHILDREN LEARN AS THEY PLAY. MOST IMPORTANTLY, IN PLAY CHILDREN LEARN HOW TO LEARN.
>
> (O. Fred Donaldson, 1993)

1.0 CHALLENGING EARLY LEARNING

The youngest of our three children recently celebrated her fourth birthday. Living in England as we do, this means she has just a few months left before she starts school. So now seems a good time to reflect on her nursery experiences.

For the last two years, Phoebe has attended two Early Years settings: an outdoor nursery and a playgroup. We wish she could attend the outdoor nursery every morning, but unfortunately it is only open twice a week. So she heads off to the local playgroup for the other three weekday mornings.

When it is a Little Acorns day, she springs out of bed and is the first one ready, waiting expectantly by the door with her rucksack on her back. (See Figure 1.) When it is a playgroup day, she gets herself ready without any fuss but without much excitement either. On arrival, she bounces off to Little Acorns without so much as a glance back or a kiss on the cheek. At the beginning of the three playgroup mornings per week, she generally holds hands with one of us until the last moment and gives us a tight hug before she enters the room. At the end of the day, she is full of chatter about the Little Acorns activities she's been engaged in, whereas we rarely get an insight into her playgroup day.

Our daughter is the same child every day. She comes from the same home with the same parents and same brother and sister. Yet she is also so very different depending on which Early Years setting she attends that day. It was the same for her older siblings. That is how significant educational settings are. Get it right, and children will flourish; just do OK, and children will just do OK.

The culture you set makes an enormous difference in the attitudes and experiences of your young learners.

The aim of this book, therefore, is to share what Little Acorns (and many other nurseries and schools just like it) are getting right in the hope that more of our young children might thrive more of the time. There is no recipe for success, of course. So much depends on context. But in our experience, there are very definitely aspects of learning in the Early Years that seem to work much better than others to encourage, nurture and excite young children, and so it is these that we will share with you here.

1.1 ENCOURAGING GROWTH IN A NURSERY

The names for Early Years settings vary so much around the world, from daycare to preschool, crèche to nursery, kindergarten to playgroup. Of these, we would like to draw attention to the term 'nursery' because of the comparison with horticultural nurseries in which young plants are nourished and grown. This might seem a strange thing to do, but bear with us, please: there is a good reason to do so.

Some people we work with, particularly in Scandinavia, view with suspicion any attempt to 'teach' or 'challenge' young children. Their belief is that youngsters should be allowed to play,

Figure 1: Phoebe Nottingham at Little Acorns

investigate and try without the direction of 'pushy' adults. They believe in a form of child-centred learning in which children should go in any (safe) direction their curiosity and interest take them. Adults should not lead.

Though we have sympathy with this ideal in that we are certainly not advocating pushiness, it is also true to say we *are* promoting the idea of adults designing specific learning opportunities for children to engage in. Not hothousing or controlling but engaging and extending children's learning. So we would like to take this opportunity to explain our point of view before we proceed with this book, and to do so, we'd like to draw a comparison with horticulture.

If we were to consider plants, it would be true to say that many species are remarkably hardy. Lay down some new concrete, and still some plant life will find a way through. Gardens that are tended lovingly still have weeds growing in unwanted places. Even with the most unforgiving of elements, vegetation finds a way to grow. Hot deserts and freezing tundra show sign of life. The hardiest always seems to find a way to survive. Naturally.

Horticulturalists know this, of course, and yet they don't just leave it to nature. They want other plants to survive too. Indeed, not just survive but thrive. So they cultivate, tend, provide for and protect their young crops to enable more of them to flourish and grow. They alter the conditions and the provisions so that even weaker saplings have a chance to bloom. They know that many plants will survive without their help, but they also know if they get the conditions just right, then many more will not just survive but also thrive.

So it is with education: children tend to learn. Naturally. Children develop socially, physically, emotionally and intellectually even when the situation is 'just OK'. Think back to the story of our youngest in the previous section: she is learning all the time, even at her uninspiring playgroup. The playgroup supervisors rarely provide super engaging activities, but Phoebe and her pals still learn. They play, they investigate; they think.

Yet at Little Acorns (the Early Years setting that excites our youngest child the most), there is a mix of free play *and* purposeful play. Free play is encouraged, of course, but there is *also* time to engage in activities, designed by the adults, that engage, extend, excite and puzzle the children. The activities are still 'child centred' in that they start from where the children are in terms of developmental levels and interest levels. But, rather like the horticulturalists, the adults are also

1. Creating the conditions for early learning

looking at ways to support each sapling's growth so that each and every one of them flourish and thrive.

Unfortunately, this analogy leads very quickly to the idea of hothousing and/or pruning to create the 'ideal' form. Of course, we are *not* advocating either of these approaches. There are already far too many people (parents and educators) falling into the trap of hothousing or 'pruning' children's interests and activities in the pursuit of 'ideal' scores in narrowly conceived, standardised tests.

Instead of hothousing or standardising, we are advocating a 'nursery' approach to learning: one in which conditions are adjusted to promote the growth and development of every single 'plant'. This might include a frame to support and extend, words of encouragement (you talk to your plants, don't you?) to nurture and show care, help for roots as well as leaf tips, moving the pots into the light or the shade, depending on the need, and so on. In other words, we are advocating small but definite adjustments to encourage growth of all young 'saplings'. In our minds, that is what will help children in in Early Years and school settings to flourish.

But then that leads to the question: learning what?

1.2 LEARNING HOW TO LEARN

What are the goals of education for young children? A lot of people ask this question and receive many more answers than they bargained for. Answers range from helping children to learn, to keeping them safe; introducing them to the values of society; encouraging a love of language; giving them the experience of socialising, harmonising and behaving appropriately; and so the list goes on.

(James): Whenever I am asked what the purpose of education is, I tend to include in my answer, 'learning how to learn'. Of course, as we've already said, children learn naturally. Watch babies 'sensing' the environment and people around them, and we can see that even the youngest beginning straightaway (and probably even before birth). And yet this ability for learning can be enhanced.

In the previous section, we compared horticulture with education, saying that by adjusting the conditions, we can help young 'saplings' to flourish and thrive. And that, I believe, is true in the case of plants *and* humans. However, one of the many differences between these two life forms is that, as humans, we also have consciousness and an awareness of self. So not only do we adapt to the environment around us, but we are also able to think about and change that very environment to suit ourselves. As far as we know, plants are not able to do that!

Amongst the many important roles that education plays is the nurturing of the emerging sense of self in young children. During their nursery years, children grow from reactive to proactive creatures. They learn that they are able to plan, design and influence the world around them. They don't just have to respond to the people and things around them; they can actually influence and sometimes control those things. And so it is with learning. Children can learn how to adapt, change, improve and control their own learning.

For example, a young child might say 'that one' when actually they mean, 'What is that?' When they don't get the response they are seeking, they begin to wonder why. Later, a different child asks, 'What is that?' and receives the response that the first child had hoped for. So now the first child reflects on this and tries out the question for themselves: success! They get the response they were after! Of course, this is just a rudimentary form of reflection but an important one nonetheless. Taking this further, as adults working with children, we can (and in my opinion should) therefore look for ways to help our young charges not just learn but also to learn how to learn.

That then leads to the question: how can we teach children how to learn? It seems to be a relatively simple question, but, of course, the answer is far more complex. Learning how to learn includes knowing how to ask meaningful questions and how to decide which answers are the best; it includes thinking about the tone and timing of interactions; and it includes when to persevere in comparison to when to compromise. The list is almost endless, and it is very definitely contextual.

Indeed, it is unlikely that any one society could agree on one set of guidelines. A national or regional government might publish a summary for local education, but that doesn't mean everyone – or indeed *anyone* – will agree completely!

We are advocating a 'nursery' approach to learning: one in which conditions are adjusted to help all 'seedlings' to flourish and bloom.

All children learn, and yet helping them learn 'how' to learn can enhance their development even further.

Learning *how* to learn includes learning how to reflect, to check, to compare and to reason.

Learning 'how' to learn is enhanced when you know which direction you wish to take your children.

That shouldn't stop us coming together in our own educational setting to agree on at least some of our aims. Indeed, it is generally worthwhile to do so because, without direction, deciding on our next steps becomes casual at best and chaotic at worst. Cast your mind back to *Alice in Wonderland* (Lewis Carroll, 1865) when Alice asks the Cheshire Cat for directions:

Alice:　　　　　　　　Would you tell me, please, which way I ought to go from here?

The Cheshire Cat:　　That depends a good deal on where you want to get to.

Alice:　　　　　　　　I don't much care where.

The Cheshire Cat:　　Then it doesn't much matter which way you go.

Alice:　　　　　　　　. . . So long as I get somewhere.

The Cheshire Cat:　　Oh, you're sure to do that, if only you walk long enough.

Thinking about what you want your children to learn by the time they leave you is an important discussion to have with your colleagues.

As the Cheshire Cat says, if you don't know where you are going, then it doesn't really matter which route you take. And yet in real life, it does matter. In our educational settings, it *does* matter where we go with our children and how we get there. It matters to the children, it matters to their parents, and it matters to us.

NOW TRY THIS

The sorts of questions that can help identify the purpose of your educational setting include:

- **What do we want our children to be capable of (for example, by the time they leave us and move onto the next stage of education)?**

- **What learning attitudes do we want our children to value and develop?**

- **What are the social and emotional behaviours we want to encourage in our children?**

We have also included a Diamond Nine activity at the end of this chapter about things that children in nursery and school should learn. This can be a good way to begin talking about what is important to you as a group or staff.

Throughout the book, there are many 'Now Try This' suggestions to help you and your colleagues reflect on your children's early learning experiences. This is the first of them.

Once you and your colleagues have thought about these questions or had a go at the Diamond Nine in Section 1.7, it can be very useful to organise your ideas into three categories: attitudes, skills and knowledge. These come together in the ASK Model. Originally written about by James in his second book, *Encouraging Learning* (2013), here is an adapted version for use with younger children.

1.3 THE ASK MODEL

ASK stands for attitudes, skills and knowledge, which are made up of these key ingredients (see Figure 2):

The ASK Model helps to identify the attitudes, skills and knowledge you would like your children to develop.

- **Attitudes**: Positive attitudes towards learning, including curiosity and willingness to try

- **Skills**: Abilities to carry out those actions necessary to accomplish something

- **Knowledge**: Familiarity with information such as facts, concepts and context

When drawn as a triangle, the ASK model can be used as a planning and reflection tool.

The ASK Model is commonly drawn as a triangle. This means that you can plot any activity along one of the sides of the triangle. Thus, if you placed an activity along the bottom line in Figure 2, then this would indicate an emphasis on (A) attitudes and (K) knowledge.

Figure 2: The ASK Model

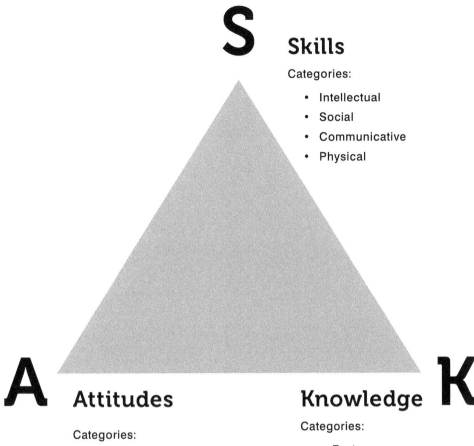

S Skills

Categories:

- Intellectual
- Social
- Communicative
- Physical

A Attitudes

Categories:

- Intellectual
- Social
- Emotional
- Moral

Knowledge K

Categories:

- Facts
- Concepts
- Ideas
- Use (e.g. of language)

For example, the purpose of a learning activity could be to consider the fairest way to divide eight pieces of chocolate among six children. This would involve the children exercising their moral attitude (A) of being fair with the knowledge (K) of how to share.

Or another example could be designing an activity to help children ask questions about a story they've just heard. So this would be a balance between the skill (S) of asking questions (an intellectual skill) and the uncovering of information or knowledge (K) about the story.

When toddlers are learning to walk, the adults around them would be likely to encourage them to keep going and not give up. In ASK Model terms, this could be said to be developing the emotional attitude (A) of determination with the physical skill (S) of walking.

Over the next few pages, we have given some examples of the attitudes and skills that you might wish to develop with your young children. These are by no means exhaustive lists. Instead, they are intended to give you some inspiration as well as to better explain what we mean by the ASK Model.

Plot a point along one side of the triangle to show which two aspects of learning are being activated.

For example, an X along the bottom of the triangle would reflect an activity that enhances an attitude (of, for example, being careful) whilst also enhancing the knowledge (for example, knowledge of hygiene).

1.4 THE ASK MODEL: ATTITUDES

Lev Vygotsky, one of the pioneers of educational psychology, wrote at length about cultural learning. He said children learn from those around them: what to laugh at, what to be afraid of, what to have a go at, what to avoid, and so on. He emphasised that children pick up mental as well as physical habits from their elders, and warned us that the way we react to things is arguably more influential on young minds than the knowledge we share with children. In other words, children adopt many of our attitudes and values through dialogue with us. That's one heck of a responsibility for those of us with children in our lives!

Of course, there is no hierarchy or exhaustive list of attitudes, at least not that we're aware of, but here are some that are displayed by the best learners we've come across. The most enthusiastic and capable learners are:

- Full of wonder.

- Curious.

- Willing to try.

- Want to learn from their mistakes.

- Focussed on what is relevant.

- Determined.

- Open to new ideas.

- Strategic.

This list shows some of the attitudes you might want to encourage in your young learners.

For an explanation of how you can help your children develop these sorts of attitudes, we encourage you to read Section 6.2, example 1.4.

Think about the differences that attitudes, skills and knowledge make to the growth and development of your children.

Compare two children you work with. List the attitudes, skills or knowledge of a child making lots of progress compared with those of a child not making much progress currently.

	Child making lots of progress	Child not making much progress
1.		
2.		
3.		
4.		
5.		

Once you have identified five differences between these two children, write down three actions that could be taken to help the less successful child make more progress.

Action 1	
Action 2	
Action 3	

1.4.1 The Marshmallow Experiment

One of the better known examples of attitudes to be encouraged in young children is that of self-control. Just mention 'the Marshmallow Experiment', and many of us in early childhood education will have at least a vague recollection of the case study.

A good example of an attitude to teach children is that of being willing to wait.

In 1972, Stanford University psychologist Walter Mischel conducted an experiment to find out when the trait of deferred gratification – the ability to wait for something you want – develops in children. The experiment has been repeated many times since, including in the BBC series *Child of Our Time* (Mischel, 2011).

The original experiment involved more than 600 children between the ages of four and six. Sitting in an empty room, the children were offered a treat of their choice – a cookie, a pretzel or a marshmallow. They were each told they could eat their treat, but if they could wait for 15 minutes without eating it, then they would get a second one. (See Figure 3.)

The Marshmallow Experiment showed how important it is to develop children's capacity for waiting.

We encourage you to watch some of the video clips of similar experiments available online. In them you'll see some children refusing to look at their marshmallow, others peeking at it from behind their hands, one boy licking the plate but not the marshmallow, and one even stroking it as if it were a pet!

In all, approximately one-third of the children were able to delay their gratification long enough to be rewarded with a second marshmallow. Of course, the older the child, the more likely he was to succeed, but what Mischel also found from follow-up studies was:

Children in the experiment who could not wait before eating their marshmallow showed higher incidences of behavioural problems later in life.

The children who could not wait were more likely to have behavioural problems both at home and school; they had lower exam scores; more often struggled to deal with stressful situations or to pay attention; and found it more difficult to maintain friendships.

The children who were able to wait also craved the treat but were able to distract themselves by covering their eyes, playing hide and seek or singing songs. Their desire wasn't dispelled; it was merely forgotten.

Whereas those who did manage to wait until they were rewarded with a second marshmallow showed higher degrees of happiness and stability in later life.

Forty years after the first experiment, the researchers tracked down 60 of the original participants and invited them to take part in a new study. They were shown a range of flash cards with faces

Figure 3: The Marshmallow Experiment

displaying a range of expressions – happy, neutral or fearful – and asked to press a button every time they saw a fearful face.

This may seem an easy task, but, as B. J. Casey, the neuropsychologist who carried out the tests along with Mischel, explains: 'A happy face is a social cue that is hard to resist'. The results showed that the participants who had struggled to defer gratification when they were younger also struggled to resist pressing the button when they saw a happy face.

The experiment concluded with many of the participants repeating the test whilst lying in a brain scanner. The participants with better self-control showed more activity in the part of the brain associated with risk aversion, whereas those with poorer self-control showed increased activity in the brain region associated with reward and addiction.

Increasing children's willingness to defer gratification can lead to significantly positive outcomes.

The outcome from this study is the recommendation that young children should be helped to develop the capacity to wait for or defer gratification. Telling them they shouldn't want something doesn't help; we can help them instead by teaching tactics to divert their attention, to focus on other things, to look forward, to plan and so on. Incidentally, this is partly why so many diets fail – we focus on the foods we shouldn't eat rather than on finding healthier foods or activities to distract us.

NOW TRY THIS

Developing the attitude of self-control

Self-control develops with maturity and practice. Temperament also plays a role. Impetuous children may need more guidance, particularly in exciting or distracting situations; reflective children may appear more self-controlled when in fact they're just more reserved. Either way, explaining the reasons behind particular rules, teaching children how to focus and appealing to their sense of fairness should help develop their attitude. Modelling self-control always helps too!

Suggested activities

1 **Tell children about exciting activities or events coming up, and then draw attention to waiting strategies they could use in the meantime.**

2   Set a medium- to long-term target with the children and engage them in collecting enough tokens to reach the 'prize'.

3   Play waiting games. For example, waiting for 10 seconds after a question has been asked before children give their answers.

4   Use daily planners to show the main activities of the day. Draw attention to some of the things the children can do whilst waiting for the more exciting events to begin.

5   Talk about the strategies you use for waiting. As you do this, model 'waiting' language such as 'yet', 'soon', 'later' and 'until' so that the children make the connection between words and actions.

6   Play games in which there is a switch in the instructions so that children need to think more before responding. This develops self-control because the children need to check their own responses rather than use auto responses. For example, play *Heads, Shoulders, Knees and Toes*, but switch the instructions so that when you say 'head', they should touch their toes, or when you say 'shoulders', they should touch their knees.

A video showing the last example in practice can be viewed at youtu.be/CVT6FQ9czoc.

1.5 THE ASK MODEL: SKILLS

As well as helping children develop learning attitudes, it is a good idea to think about the skills children need for learning. Here's a list to begin with. It is not exhaustive, but it will give you a reference point and underpins some of the activities later in the book.

This list shows some of the categories of skills you might want to encourage in your young learners.

Intellectual skills – including the ability to:

- Concentrate.
- Remember.
- Make connections.
- Understand an idea.
- Give opinions.
- Ask questions.

Social skills – including the ability to:

- Make friends.
- Understand other people have different ideas.
- Respond appropriately to others.
- Work individually and in a team.
- Encourage others.
- Influence others.

Communication skills – including the ability to:

- Communicate clearly.
- Listen to others.
- Respond appropriately.
- Request things politely.
- Understand body language and tone of voice.
- Choose a good time to talk.

Physical skills – including the ability to:

- Write, draw and paint.
- Manipulate objects (e.g. building a model with LEGO).
- Catch and throw objects.
- Dance, act, sing.
- Balance and ride (e.g. on a bike or scooter).
- Climb, sit still, play a sport.

Of course, many of these skills overlap. Writing, painting and drawing are intellectual as well as physical skills. We have suggested some activities in Chapter 4 for developing learning skills and attitudes with children. However, the most important thing is to think about and look for ways to enhance children's attitudes and skills as well as their knowledge. By getting the balance right, you will give children a great head start.

1.6 LEARNING DETECTIVES

Learning Detectives is an idea created by our former colleague, Louise Brown. She developed the approach as a way to help her four- and five-year-old children think about what they are learning. We have also written about adaptations of it in *Challenging Learning Through Dialogue* (Nottingham, Nottingham, Renton, 2017) and *Challenging Learning Through Feedback* (Nottingham & Nottingham, 2017).

The Learning Detectives approach helps children concentrate on 'how' to learn.

Learning Detectives are children who have been nominated to stay 'outside' of the main learning task. Their job is to look for 'clues' of learning such as listening, asking questions, concentrating, remembering, taking turns and so on. Over the next few pages, you will find example clues together with visual prompts for the children. In our experience, this approach works well with children from the age of four onwards.

A good way to introduce Learning Detectives is to say to your children something along the lines of: 'Wow, you've learnt so many things already. You've learnt to walk and talk; to ask for things; to make friends; to ride a scooter. How on earth did you manage to do all of that?'

The children are likely to say, 'We tried hard', to which you can reply, 'Well, that is an important thing to do when learning. So, let's make that one of our Learning Detective clues. Now, what else helped you to learn to walk and talk and make friends?' They then might say, 'Getting help'. You can then add this to your list of clues for the children to detect. By doing this, you create a starter list that can be built on as the year progresses.

There are many ways to use Learning Detectives. This list gives a few examples.

What you do next will depend on the developmental stage of the children. Here are some possibilities:

1. Select between one and four children to be Learning Detectives.

2. Give them a prop to show that they have been chosen as a detective: this could be a hat, a magnifying glass, a notepad, a camera or simply the clue they are looking for on a piece of card.

3. Print a selection of the cards shown on the next few pages, and give each Learning Detective one clue each.

4. Ask each detective to look for examples of her 'clue'. For example, if she got the 'listening' card, then she should look for incidences of other children listening.

5. The Learning Detectives should record the incidences of their clues in action. For example, they might write down the name of the person they saw listening. Or they might take a photograph of the person listening. Or they might point out that person to an adult.

The children you choose to be Learning Detectives look for 'clues' of learning such as thinking, listening, asking questions, etc.

Once the Learning Detectives have collected some examples of the clue they are looking for, then you should bring all the children (the Learning Detectives *and* the other children) together to consider the findings. This is a really important part of the process.

When you have gathered the children together, ask the Learning Detectives to reveal the clues that they were searching for and the examples they found. For example, the Learning Detective who was looking for examples of listening should tell the rest of the children what they were looking for and whom they saw doing some really good listening.

Then you should question their findings to give them more opportunity to articulate their thinking. For example:

You:	What learning clue were you searching for?
Child:	Listening.
You:	What does that mean?
Child:	Using your ears.
You:	So, who was listening?
Child:	Sarah and John were listening.
You:	How do you know that?
Child:	Because they were looking at the person who was talking.
You:	But do we listen by looking?
Child:	No, we listen with our ears.
You:	So why would is it a good idea to look at the person who is talking?
Child:	Because then they know you are listening because they can see you are.

(James): Incidentally, the answers given in this dialogue represent a real-life interaction I had with a group of four-year-old Learning Detectives recently. In my opinion, the children were trying to explain the importance of encouraging a speaker by showing that you are listening. Of course, the children didn't have the language skills yet to explain precisely, but I think you can tell that they were at least giving it their best shot.

Anyway, the point of asking these questions is *not* to try to catch the children out. In fact, the very opposite is true: the aim is to support the children's learning by helping them to articulate their ideas. It is also to give the other children the opportunity to understand what is meant by terms such as listening, concentrating, taking turns and so on. Many children already know what these words mean, but others might not be so sure, which is why it is important to unpack the terms with the children.

The impact of children not fully understanding what is meant by terms such as these can be seen frequently in educational settings. For example, ask young children in a primary school in England who is listening, and you will see most children covering their lips with their index finger. See Figure 4 for a prime example of this. If you look at that picture, the boy does indeed look as though he is paying attention and listening to the teacher. However, some children – perhaps even in that same class – think his finger-on-lips pose is enough to 'prove' he is listening. This then leads to some children placing a finger on their own lips but continuing to talk and distract others. They then react indignantly when someone tells them that they are not listening! 'Of course, I'm listening', they assert: 'I've got a finger over my lips!'

We suspect the reason for this is that teachers very often 'shush' young children in the hope of quietening them down, and they do this by putting their index finger to their lips. Some of the more attentive children copy this and get praised for it. So other children copy them by putting their fingers on their lips also, but very many of them don't realise that they also have to stop talking and start concentrating!

Being clear is the key here, and talking through the Learning Detective findings can help enormously.

For more ideas about how to help your children learn the most from the Learning Detectives strategy, we encourage you to read Section 6.2, example 1.6.

Once the Learning Detectives have collected their clues, bring all your children together to review the findings.

Encouraging your children to talk about their findings and question the meanings of each clue will help to deepen everyone's understanding of learning behaviours.

The Learning Detective cards in Figure 5 can be used as prompts for your children. Depending on their age, you could give each child between one and five clues to look for at any one time.

Figure 4: Fingers on lips to show you are listening

1.7 CHAPTER SUMMARY

This chapter has covered the following main points:

1   Every educational setting has a culture all of its own; what culture do you want yours to have?

2   As well as free play, we are advocating that early learning also includes specially designed learning activities that extend, excite and engage young children.

3   Nurseries for children have something in common with 'nurseries' for plants: both cultivate, tend, provide for and protect their young to enable more of them to flourish and grow.

4   The ASK Model can help to shape and organise learning for your nursery children.

5   The Learning Detectives strategy is a great way to help children think and talk about their learning.

The cards in Figure 6 are there to help you with this reflection activity.

NOW TRY THIS

With your colleagues, place the cards in Figure 6 into a Diamond Nine to show which Learning Intentions are most important (place them towards the top) and which are least important (place them towards the bottom). An example Diamond Nine is shown in Figure 14 (page 38).

Figure 5: Learning Detective cards

Agreeing

©2017 www.challenginglearning.com

Concentrating

©2017 www.challenginglearning.com

Observing

©2017 www.challenginglearning.com

Sharing ideas

©2017 www.challenginglearning.com

Experimenting

©2017 www.challenginglearning.com

Thinking

©2017 www.challenginglearning.com

Pretending

©2017 www.challenginglearning.com

Imagining

©2017 www.challenginglearning.com

Helping others with their learning

©2017 www.challenginglearning.com

ACTIVITY:
Figure 5: Learning Detective Cards
1-19

Exploring

©2017 www.challenginglearning.com

ACTIVITY:
Figure 5: Learning Detective Cards
1-20

Showing

©2017 www.challenginglearning.com

ACTIVITY:
Figure 5: Learning Detective Cards
1-21

Solving problems

©2017 www.challenginglearning.com

ACTIVITY:
Figure 5: Learning Detective Cards
1-22

Asking for help

©2017 www.challenginglearning.com

ACTIVITY:
Figure 5: Learning Detective Cards
1-23

Inventing games

©2017 www.challenginglearning.com

ACTIVITY:
Figure 5: Learning Detective Cards
1-24

Being sensitive to others

©2017 www.challenginglearning.com

ACTIVITY:
Figure 5: Learning Detective Cards
1-25

Following instructions

©2017 www.challenginglearning.com

ACTIVITY:
Figure 5: Learning Detective Cards
1-26

Giving instructions

©2017 www.challenginglearning.com

ACTIVITY:
Figure 5: Learning Detective Cards
1-27

Finding information

©2017 www.challenginglearning.com

Figure 6: Sample Learning Intentions

ACTIVITY: Figure 6: Early Learning Goals 1-1 **Learn to make friends** ©2017 www.challenginglearning.com	ACTIVITY: Figure 6: Early Learning Goals 1-2 **Learn to walk, run and jump** ©2017 www.challenginglearning.com	ACTIVITY: Figure 6: Early Learning Goals 1-3 **Count accurately from 1-20** ©2017 www.challenginglearning.com
ACTIVITY: Figure 6: Early Learning Goals 1-4 **Explain ideas and ask questions** ©2017 www.challenginglearning.com	ACTIVITY: Figure 6: Early Learning Goals 1-5 **Show appropriate emotions** ©2017 www.challenginglearning.com	ACTIVITY: Figure 6: Early Learning Goals 1-6 **Develop confidence** ©2017 www.challenginglearning.com
ACTIVITY: Figure 6: Early Learning Goals 1-7 **Listen attentively to others** ©2017 www.challenginglearning.com	ACTIVITY: Figure 6: Early Learning Goals 1-8 **Recognise and describe patterns** ©2017 www.challenginglearning.com	ACTIVITY: Figure 6: Early Learning Goals 1-9 **Manage own personal hygiene** ©2017 www.challenginglearning.com

2. CHILDREN'S RESPONSE TO CHALLENGE

> IT IS EASIER TO BUILD STRONG CHILDREN THAN
> TO REPAIR BROKEN MEN.
>
> (Frederick Douglass, 1964)

2.0 WHICH PATH WOULD YOU CHOOSE?

We invite you to show the image in Figure 7 to your children and then ask them which path they would choose. Happily, most children in early childhood go for the one on the right.

Unfortunately though, as children grow older, more and more of them pick the easier option – particularly when that choice is between two learning tasks rather than two paths through the woods.

We ask you to consider the 'paths question' because of something we first read in John Hattie's seminal book, *Visible Learning* (2009):

> The effect of student choice and control over learning is somewhat higher on motivation outcomes (d = 0.30) than on subsequent student learning (d = 0.04; Niemiec, Sikorski, & Walberg, 1996; Patall, Cooper, & Robinson, 2008).
>
> (p. 193)

Research shows that when children are given choice, too many of them pick the easier option. This can then reduce the amount of learning that takes place.

Bearing in mind, the typical effect of *all* factors influencing student achievement is an effect size of 0.4, then the effect of giving children choice shows just how pitifully small 0.04 is. Indeed, you could say that giving children choice slows down their rate of learning!

Which path would you choose?

Figure 7: The path to challenge

Let's be careful here: Hattie is not saying, 'Do not give children choice'. Instead, his analysis of thousands of studies begs the questions why would giving children choice result in increased motivation but *decreased* learning? and, perhaps more importantly, what can we do about it?

When we first read this statistic, our reaction was to think: 'What a load of rubbish! That can't be true. Or if it is, then it must apply to school-aged only students because in the Early Years, children are always given choice and yet they seem to learn lots'.

Yet let's look back at Figure 7 and consider this: if the left-hand path represents an activity that children can do easily and the right-hand path represents something that looks challenging, then how many children might gravitate towards the easier one?

Even young children are prone to picking the activities they know they are good at, aren't they? Those who can already ride gravitate towards bike riding; those who are able to use paint brushes better than others head towards the painting activities; and those who are articulate and confident are more likely to engage in social play. In other words, if children are already competent at something, they do it again and again. Whereas if they don't think they're very good at something, then they are less likely to have a go unless guided or encouraged by others.

So, in other words, if children gravitate towards those things that they can do, then perhaps we shouldn't be surprised that they don't learn as much as when they try something that is out of their comfort zone.

NOW TRY THIS

Before we get into this further, please take the opportunity to think why children go for the things that they can do rather than the things they can't do yet.

Reason 1

Reason 2

Reason 3

2.1 WHY DO CHILDREN PICK THE EASIER PATH?

A lot of our work is in Scandinavia, and there they use the term 'curling parents' to describe parents who 'smooth' the path to help their little darlings go further! Perhaps *that* is why children are less adventurous than they used to be: because of their *curling parents*? (See Figure 8.) Certainly a generation or two ago, most children would spend carefree days playing outside with

Figure 8: Curling parents

not an adult in sight. Nowadays, so many more are chaperoned from one organised activity to another, under the watchful eye of a responsible adult. And if ever children are 'let loose', they always have to take a mobile phone with them so that they can send regular updates as to their whereabouts. No wonder children are becoming more and more dependent upon their curling parents!

Yet perhaps it is too easy to blame parents, and, to be honest, this book is not about changes in society anyway; it is about education for three- to seven-year-olds. So let's consider what goes on in our own setting instead. How much 'curling' do we get involved in? How often is it that we look for ways to make things more straightforward for our young charges? We see a child struggling to accomplish something, so we give him a helping hand. There's a child about to make a mistake, so we intervene to make sure she gets it right the first time. There's a group trying to decide who should go first, second or third, so we swoop in to make the decision for them because it's easier to do so!

Of course, we are not saying adults should never help children – far from it! What we are wondering, though, is whether one of the reasons why so many children pick the easier option is because they have learnt that adults just want them to get it right. They see that adults congratulate children when they get it right and commiserate with them when they get it wrong. So the choice now becomes do you want to be praised for what you've done well, or do you want to receive feedback for how you could improve?

As children grow older, this state of affairs seems to be exacerbated even more. Ask students in school which of these scores they are more likely to be praised for:

$$6/10 \qquad 10/10$$

Most children will, of course, say, ten out of ten. Now ask them in which activity they are most likely to get ten out of ten, and they will indicate whichever task they think is the easiest one for them.

So yet again, they are encouraged to select the easy path.

Also think about when students in school are confused or make mistakes: how often do their teachers help to correct the mistakes in a confidential manner so as not to show the students up in front of their friends? Of course, it is a good thing that fewer teachers these days go down the public humiliation route, but consider what the underlying message of the clandestine approach is: mistakes are something to be ashamed of, so I will protect your ego by helping you quietly.

Before you worry that we are advocating a return to the naming and shaming approach that too many of us encountered in our youth: we are not! We are saying that there are better ways to go

Curling parents are those parents who want to make their children's 'paths' smoother and less problematic.

It's not just parents who smooth the way for their children; a lot of adults in Early Years settings and schools do the same thing too.

Which of these two scores are children more likely to be praised for?

If children think they are more likely to be praised for getting things right, then they are more likely to lean towards easier activities.

about things. Some of these will be covered in depth in Section 5.1. For now, though, we want to make the point that if mistakes are treated as something to be embarrassed about, then yet again we encourage children to take the easier, less problematic path.

(James): Recently, we went on a family bike ride. Our three-year-old sat on the back of my bike and never stopped talking the whole journey! Our ten-year-old jumped on her bike, and away she pedalled confidently. Our seven-year-old had just got a new bike for his birthday, and you know how that goes: buy a frame that's a bit too big so that the bike will last longer! So on he jumps and away he wobbles! He keeps going, but he wobbles way more than my heart would have liked.

As we were cycling, I asked myself which one is learning the most about bike riding on this journey? The answer, of course, is my son Harry. He was out of his comfort zone and was therefore having to concentrate more than his sisters. He was learning how to handle a bigger bike; he was learning more about balancing. He was learning about using gears (this was the first bike he'd ever ridden that had more than one gear). Our girls were enjoying the ride, but they were not learning nearly as much as their brother was.

Think about driving your car. When you drive from home to work every day, you can do so almost on autopilot. You don't have to think about your driving because it comes easily to you now. Yet think about driving somewhere completely different: perhaps a busy city in a foreign country where they drive on the 'wrong' side of the road! How much more would you have to concentrate? How much more would you be learning then?

Back to the bike riding: what would you have thought of me as a father if I had said to Harry: 'Son, I think you're wobbling too much. Why don't you get off and walk? Or why don't I ask your sister to run alongside you, holding the frame so that you don't wobble too much?' If I had done that, then no doubt you would have thought, there goes one of those curling parents that the Scandinavians talk about! Or how about when you're driving in a foreign city, your fellow passengers bombard you with unsolicited advice about what not to do? Just how welcome are those back-seat drivers?

The thing is: how often do we engage in a bit of back-seat driving or curling parenting in our early childhood settings? When a child is struggling to get something right, how many of us rush to his aide? When a child is not in full control, how often do we 'walk alongside her' in the hope of giving them encouragement and support? We even plan activities for children that are based on what are they going to be able to achieve by the end of the morning rather than what is going to make them wobble. Not always, of course, but often and perhaps too often.

Again: what is the message we send to children when we do exactly that: when we walk alongside them, lead them, or stop them from wobbling? We might be saying that we are here to help, but, unfortunately, we are also saying: it is not great being out of your comfort zone. Better to play it safe and get it right than to challenge yourself and risk getting it wrong. No wonder so many children pick the easier path when given the choice!

When we teach children to ride a bicycle, we give them lots of praise when they are in the learning phase. When they are out of their comfort zone and wobbling (but not giving up) is exactly the right time to encourage them most.

It is the same in education: we should praise our children most when they are struggling with something but not giving up. This is far better than praising children for doing something that they can already do.

NOW TRY THIS

Randomly select three times over the next week in your setting. For example, 10 a.m. Monday, 12.30 p.m. Wednesday and 2 p.m. Thursday. At each of those times, count up the number of children choosing to engage in an activity that they can already do compared to the number of children choosing to have a go at something that is out of their comfort zone.

Talk about the findings with your colleagues, answering the following questions:

1 **What does the number of children choosing the easy path compared to the challenging path tell you about their attitude towards learning?**

2 **What surprises you about your findings?**

3 **What could you do next to encourage even more children to choose to step out of their comfort zone more of the time?**

2.2 PERSUADING CHILDREN TO STEP OUT OF THEIR COMFORT ZONE

The story about the family bike ride involved just three children, and, even then, only one of them was out of his comfort zone. In our educational settings, we have way more than three children! So how on earth do we get all of *them* out of their comfort zone?

That is why we began this chapter by talking about children's choices. If we can persuade children that the better choice is the more challenging option, then we won't have to do all the leading ourselves; the children will seek out the opportunities for themselves. For example, suppose our eldest daughter had said to us on the bike ride, 'Can I go on the mountain bike trail please and then see you at the other end?' or 'Can I have a go at riding your bike, Dad?' or even, 'Can I try riding a stunt bike so that I can try different tricks?' Then we (the adults) will not need to be the ones having to think all the time about how to challenge our children. Instead, the children will look for ways to challenge themselves. In other words, when children are given choices in future, their learning will increase because they pick the challenging option rather than decrease because, as the research suggests, they pick the easier option.

If we encourage and praise children most when they are out of their comfort zone, then we give the impression that the challenging option is the better one to choose.

Cast your mind back to the advert that began with a time-lapse video showing just how many more people chose to ride the escalators rather than walk up the stairs from a metro station? The advertisers then made the steps much more appealing by transforming them into a keyboard so that people using the stairs would end up playing a tune. Of course, the balance shifted immediately so that many more people took the stairs rather than the escalators from then on, to the benefit of their health.

Imagine if we could do that in our settings: make the 'healthier' option (i.e. the one that children learn most from) the more appealing one.

A good starting point for this is to break the link between challenge and 'difficulty'. Not just children but far too many people associate challenge with difficulty. If we say to children, 'I'm going to challenge you', then far too many of them take that to mean, 'I'm going to make things much more difficult for you. Mwa ha ha ha!' To which they think, 'No thanks! I think I'll give that one a miss!' Indeed, just how many of us are hoping that this year will be much more difficult for us than last year was? We suspect not many would *choose* that!

To encourage your children to pick the more challenging options, do not describe them as 'difficult'.

So let's start our young children off in the best way possible and persuade them that challenging is not the same as difficult. Instead, let's persuade children that:

Instead, describe the challenging options are more 'interesting'.

> Easy is boring; challenge is interesting.

Refer back to Figure 7. If we ask children which path looks more difficult, then they will all pick the one on the right. If however, we say which one looks more 'interesting', then, even though they will still pick the one on the right, very many more of them will be more inclined to try it out. Interesting is far more attractive than difficult, isn't it?

So, when we see children doing something easily, then we could say, 'Wow, you're finding this really easy aren't you? Shall we make it more interesting?' The children are likely to say yes because most people like things to be interesting. So then you increase the difficulty of the task! You don't call it difficult; you call it more interesting, but it's the same thing: persuading children that the path on the right is the better one to take. Only this time, you are also making it more attractive by calling it the 'interesting' option, so that later on, when faced with a choice, the children will be more likely to look for other, more 'interesting' options.

When you see children picking the easier options again and again, then say, 'Why don't we make this more interesting?' (and then make it more challenging for them).

As for the children who are already wobbling, don't rush to their aid. Instead, do as we all do when teaching children to ride bikes: encourage them to keep going. Praise them for persevering. Tell them how impressed we are that they are wobbling and not giving up. And when at last they do succeed, draw attention to the progress they have made and the achievements have earned through their own endeavours.

When children are 'wobbling', then show how delighted you are that they are willing to get out of their comfort zone and try really 'interesting' things.

This will not change attitudes overnight, but it will be a step in the right direction. Indeed, talking of 'steps', think about the change in behaviour of people who get one of those exercise monitors: they start looking for opportunities to take more steps. Rather than take the escalators, they take the stairs; rather than circle around and around in their car looking for a parking spot closest to the front door, they park further away and add a few more steps to their tally. Travelling from one gate to another in a large airport, they look for places to walk rather than travellators to ride.

In other words, if we change the goal, then the behaviour follows suit. If our goal is to arrive at our destination as efficiently as possible, then we look for the path of least resistance: whereas, if our goal is to get fitter, then we seek out opportunities for exercise. And so it is with education: if our goal is to help children succeed as painlessly as possible, then we look for every opportunity to guide, support and show; whereas if our goal is to help our children learn as much as possible, then we look for opportunities to encourage, challenge and wobble.

That is not to say that success is a bad thing, of course; it is generally a very good thing. Instead, what we are saying is that a focus on completing the task might lend itself to the adult doing it for the child (think how many parents do their children's homework for them just so that it's out of the way!); whereas, a focus on seeking out the learning opportunities might not be as efficient in terms of completing tasks quickly, but, in the long term, it is a far more effective way to help young children to grow and flourish.

Get it right now, and we will stand our children in very good stead for later in their lives. Just think how many teenagers are being squeezed by the pressure of grades, and how many of their teachers feel obliged to cover the curriculum as efficiently as possible. Think how so many school and college students think the purpose of education is to 'get the job done' rather than to engage in learning for the sake of learning.

Thankfully, early childhood hasn't gone down that path. Not yet anyway. So, before it's too late, let's remind ourselves that it is better to learn lots than it is to complete the task as quickly as possible. Let's teach our young children that trying new things, making mistakes, getting out of our comfort zone, wobbling for a while are what make learning so much fun! Proving is good but improving is even better.

2.3 THE LEARNING CHALLENGE

The Learning Challenge is one way to help children talk about being out of their comfort zone.

The Learning Challenge is designed to help children think and talk about their learning. In some ways, it is a child-friendly representation of Vygotsky's Zone of Proximal Development (1978) in that it describes the move from actual to potential understanding. It can help develop a growth mindset (Dweck, 2006), and it can encourage learners to willingly step outside their comfort zone.

(James): I created the Learning Challenge in 2003 to give my students at the time a way to describe being out of their comfort zone without feeling bad about it. Even though I had talked a lot with them about wobbling being good because it means you're improving and that mistakes are not something to be ashamed of because they are actually opportunities to learn, still many of my children felt bashful about admitting that they were struggling. So I had to find a metaphor to describe this situation in such a way that there would be no feelings of guilt or failure. So the Learning Challenge was born. I have written about it in depth in *The Learning Challenge: How to Guide Your Students Through the Learning Pit* (Nottingham, 2017). However, that book was aimed at school and college teachers, so here is the model presented for use with younger children.

At the heart of the Learning Challenge is the 'pit'. When children are 'in the pit', they are 'wobbling' with ideas or activities.

At the heart of the Learning Challenge is 'the pit'. A child could be said to be 'in the pit' when he is in a state of cognitive conflict. That is to say, when he has two or more ideas that make sense to him but, when compared side by side, appear to be in conflict with each other.

Deliberately and strategically creating a state of cognitive conflict in the minds of learners is at the heart of the Learning Challenge.

Examples of cognitive conflicts that commonly arise during Learning Challenge with young children include:

- Adults tell us to be nice to everyone but not to talk to strangers.

- It is bad to tell lies, but I told a lie to be kind.

- A toy is something that we play with, but not everything we play with is a toy (for example, we play with our friends).

- A friend is nice, but if a stranger is nice to me, then she is still not my friend.

- Stealing means taking things that are not yours, but when we go on a scavenger hunt, the adults challenge us to find as many objects as possible.

- Sweets are bad for me, but they make me feel good.

- We should think for ourselves, but adults tell us to do as we are told.

- An adult told me to make friends with that other child, but I don't think he is a very nice boy.

- I am a boy and I really like the colour pink, but some people say that pink is a girl's colour.

- My mum is always telling my older brother to stop playing on his phone, but my mum plays on her phone all the time.

- It is greedy to eat too much, but my dad says I should finish all the food on my plate.

When children think through these or other examples of cognitive conflicts, then they are 'in the pit'. This metaphor works well because it is the same as being out of their comfort zone, with being *un*comfortable. Though some people have suggested that a mountain might be less negative, in our opinion that metaphor doesn't work so well. When someone is at the top of a mountain, she can see for miles around and choose her next route with ease. Whereas when you are wobbling out of your comfort zone, then you have the sense of confusion you would feel when you're in a pit, not the one of clarity you would have at the top of a mountain. So a Learning Pit it is!

When children think through these sorts of conflicting messages, then they could be said to be 'in the pit'.

It is important to note that children are not in the pit if they have *no* idea. The pit represents moving beyond a single, basic idea into the situation of having many ideas that are as yet unsorted. So it is not when a child says 'I don't know' when we ask him what it means to be fair; it is when he thinks being fair is about giving everyone the same thing, yet at the same time realising that giving everyone the same thing isn't always fair. For example, if only one child in a group has been kind, then it wouldn't be fair to give all of the children in the group a reward – so what would be fair? If your children are thinking through lots of possibilities and haven't yet reached a conclusion, then they are definitely in the pit!

Being 'in the pit' does not mean you have 'no idea'; it means you have lots of ideas that are conflicting with one another.

The Learning Challenge is shown in Figure 9. More colourful versions are available online, as well as the one shown in Figures 26 and 27 (pages 48 and 49), but this is the original one, so this will be the one we start with.

The Learning Challenge works very well with the SOLO Taxonomy. This is covered in depth in Section 6.3. We have also shown an example of how you can help your children develop an understanding of concepts such as 'real' in Section 6.2, example 2.3.

Figure 9: The Learning Challenge

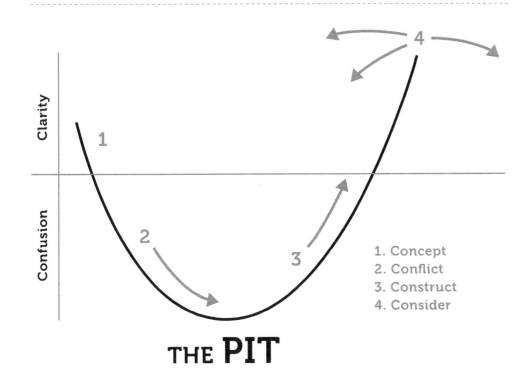

1. Concept
2. Conflict
3. Construct
4. Consider

THE **PIT**

2.4 LEARNING CHALLENGE STAGE 1: IDENTIFY CONCEPTS

The Learning Challenge begins with a concept, theme or idea.

The Learning Challenge begins with a concept. Concepts such as being nice, dreaming, pets, friends, shape, superheroes and health work very well with young children. A full list is shown in Section 2.5.3.

When your children have a basic understanding of one or more of these concepts, then they are ready to get into the pit. This tends to happen from about the age of three onwards.

Having a concept of something means being able to recognise that 'thing' and being able to distinguish it from other 'things'. The question 'How old am I?' is a factual question, whereas the question 'Am I old?' is a conceptual question because it invites the exploration of meanings, uses and interpretations. That is what makes concepts so interesting and why we need a concept to begin a Learning Challenge journey with.

The concept of 'real' is a good one to use with young children.

A good example concept to begin with is 'real'. What is meant by real, and how is it different from make-believe or pretend? The sorts of questions that engage young children in thoughts about real include:

- If I pretend to be a superhero, then would I be a real superhero?
- Is it just the things that we can see that are real?
- Are invisible things real (for example, air)?
- Is it just living things that are real? (What about a tree that is chopped up into sticks?)
- Is everything that moves or can be moved real?
- Are rainbows real?
- When you look in a mirror, is your reflection real?
- Are lies real?
- What is the difference between a real friend and an imaginary friend?
- In what ways are toys real?

Of course, props are almost always a good way to engage young children. So, for example, you could show any of the pairs of photographs in Figure 10 and ask your children to decide which ones are real and which ones are not.

One of the best ways to choose a concept is through the educere approach to learning. *Educere* is the root word in Latin from which the word 'education' comes from. Its original meaning is 'to draw out'. So rather than giving your children a concept to begin with, you could encourage them to 'draw out' concepts from a suitable stimulus such as a story, image, object or experience.

The Learning Challenge can only work if your children have at least a basic understanding of the concept before they begin.

Remember: the Learning Challenge should begin with a concept that your children understand enough for them to engage in some cognitive conflict about. If they have 'no idea' about a concept, then there will be nothing to conflict with, and therefore you will not be able to take them into the pit. This means the educere approach of getting your children to draw out concepts from a stimulus is doubly effective: not only will their involvement generate a sense of ownership, but it will also show you which concepts your children are ready to engage with.

That said, your children might understand several concepts better than it seems at first glance. For example, a lot of young children don't know how to use a ruler to measure something. Yet if we tried to start a race with some children standing much further forward than others, then they would all say that that was unfair. So even though they might not realise that measurement always should begin at zero, they will understand the concept of beginning at the same place.

A great place to find concepts that children understand is in picture books.

Our favourite source for drawing out concepts with young children is picture books. They are generally so packed full of ideas and concepts that perhaps their only real drawback is that there might be too many in one book. Even the front cover of some of these books can be enough to draw out as many as 10–15 concepts.

The books in Figure 11 are a good starting point for drawing out concepts. Remember: you are looking for concepts that your children will want to think about and that lend themselves to lots of interesting questions.

Figure 10: Which one is real?

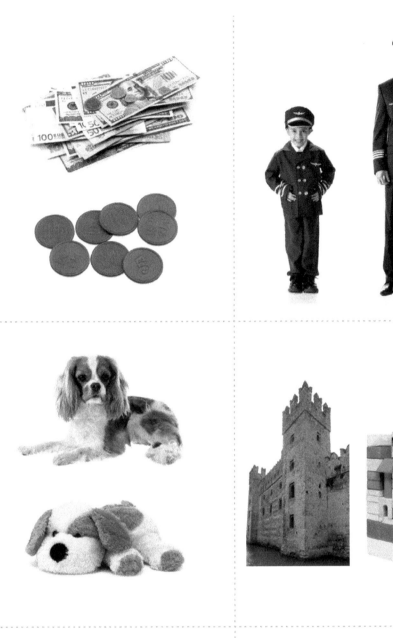

Here are a few of our favourite picture books for drawing out concepts. There are even more suggestions in the Appendix.

Figure 11: Drawing concepts out of picture books

Book details	Concepts	Age	Overview and potential questions
Not a Box **Antionette Portis**	Imagination Pretend Play Real Lies Experience	4+	A story about a bunny that has lots of fun with a cardboard box. Using his imagination, Bunny makes it clear that the box can become whatever he wants it to be. • Can you imagine absolutely anything? • Is it always good to pretend? • Is pretending the same as playing? • Is it dangerous to imagine doing something dangerous? • If you pretend to be happy, then are you really happy?
The Owl Who Was Afraid of the Dark **Jill Tomlinson**	Fear Imagination Being frightened Animals Being different	3+	Plop, the Baby Barn Owl, is afraid of the dark. Through lots of different inspiring encounters, he realises that darkness is exciting after all. • Why are some people afraid of the dark? • Can you stop yourself from being frightened? • Is it sometimes nice to be scared? • Plop is encouraged to investigate the noises he hears. Was that a good idea?
The Teddy Robber **Ian Beck** *Corgi Children's Books*	Forgiveness Ownership Reasons Stealing Toys Sharing	3+	Someone is stealing teddies. But who could it be? Who is the Teddy Robber? When Tom's own teddy is snatched in the dead of night, he is determined to get to the bottom of the mystery. • What does it mean to steal something? • If someone has a good reason to steal, does that make it OK? • If you give it back after you have taken it, does that mean it is not stealing? • Are some things OK to steal? • If we all shared everything with each other, would that put an end to stealing?
Flop Ear **Guido Van Genechten**	Being different Being the same Name-calling Teasing	3+	Flop Ear the bunny rabbit has one floppy ear. All the other bunnies make fun of him, so he tries everything to correct it: sticking a carrot in his ear, hanging upside down and tying a balloon to it. But nothing works, so, fed up with being teased, Flop Ear goes to see the doctor, who tells him it's fine to be different. On his return to the warren, all the other bunnies rejoice that he's back and try to make their ears floppy. • Should we all try to be the same? • What is good about being different? • Is it OK to have fun if it makes someone sad? • What would it be like if we all looked the same?
The Best Bottom **Brigitte Minne** *Macmillan*	Arguing Competition Fair Name-calling Best	3+	All the farm animals decide to have a competition to find the best bottom in the farmyard. Whilst they're all grooming their bottoms, they begin to argue and then to fight. Meanwhile, a frog who'd recently hopped into the farmyard and assumed he couldn't enter the competition because he didn't have a tail (and what is a bottom without a tail?) straps a bouquet of flowers to his bottom and takes first prize. • Is it OK to want to be better than others? • Are competitions good? • What does being the best mean? • Is it fair to be better than someone else?

Book details	Concepts	Age	Overview and potential questions
Where's My Teddy? **Jez Albrough** *Candlewick Press*	Being scared Comfort Frightening Lost and found Love Size	3+	Whilst Eddie's looking for his lost teddy, he comes across a very large teddy bear in the woods. Then he spots a gigantic bear with a tiny teddy. The big bear and Eddie both realise they've got each other's teddies, but, being scared of each other, they grab their own teddy and run back to their own beds, where they cuddle up close to their teddies. • Do we all need cuddles? • What makes something scary? • Are big things scarier than little things? • What makes something less scary? • What does being frightened feel like? • Are we all scared of something?
Room on the Broom **Julia Donaldson and Axel Scheffler** *Campbell Books*	Magic Friendship Helping others Real and not real Scariness	3+	This is the story of a good-natured witch and her cat that collect other friends as they fly through the sky on their broomstick. A good general stimulus with enough concepts to stimulate the novice and experienced inquirers. • Is it always a good thing to help others? • What makes this witch a good witch? • Is magic real? • Should we always be nice to one another? • Is it OK to scare someone if it is helping someone else?
The Rainbow Fish **Marcus Pfister** *North South Books*	Beauty Popularity Friendship	4+	The Rainbow Fish is the most beautiful fish in the sea, but he has no friends because he is just too beautiful to play with any of the others. The wise octopus tells him to share his beauty with the other fish in order to make friends. The Rainbow Fish gives away his shiny scales one by one but gains a sense of satisfaction from pleasing others as well as gaining a group of new friends. • What does beautiful mean? • Is it important to please other people? • What makes something beautiful? • How important is it that other people like you? • Should you share your things with others to make them like you?
The Little Red Hen	Working hard Fairness Reward Helping Sharing	3+	The little red hen finds a grain of wheat and asks for help from the other farmyard animals to plant it, but none of them volunteer. She later asks for help to harvest the wheat, mill the wheat into flour and baking the flour into bread. At each stage, no animal will help her. Finally, the hen has completed her task and asks who will help her eat the bread. This time, all the animals eagerly volunteer. She declines their help, stating that no one helped her with any of the other stages, and she eats it herself. • Why should we help others? • Should we only get a prize or reward for working hard? • Is it fair that only the hen ate the bread? • Should we always share what we have with others?
The Important Book **M. W. Brown and L. Weisgard** *Harper Collins*	Change Identity Important	3+	The pattern of the book is that the writer suggests various things like rain, a spoon or a daisy. For each item, the writer lists some qualities or purposes and gives an opinion as to the most important. The book ends on the subject of 'you'. • What does being important mean? • Is everything important? • What makes some things more important than others? • What makes you, you? • If you had a different name, would you still be you?

Another activity you could do on the concept of 'real' is to ask your children to place the cards shown in Figure 12 into two hoops. Label one hoop 'Real' and the other 'Not Real'.

Which of these images show things that are real and which ones show things that are not real?

Figure 12: Real or not real?

Ideas

Dreams

Photographs

Fruit

Pets

Friends

Car

Toy cars

A smile

A book

The sound of an owl

A cat purr

2.5 LEARNING CHALLENGE STAGE 2: CREATE COGNITIVE CONFLICT

Once your children have started talking about the chosen concept, then you should try to create some cognitive conflict in their minds.

Cognitive conflict is when people have a conflict between two ideas that they agree with but that are contradictory. So, for example, we might teach children that stealing is wrong whilst also saying that Robin Hood was a good man or that pets are animals we keep in our home but that some people have horses and pigs as pets, and they don't keep them in their homes.

It is the tension between these conflicting ideas that causes children (and adults) to think harder and longer about the concept. In other words, this is what causes them to go into the pit.

(James): If you look at youtu.be/jZ4iNeNtLOM, you will see a short video of me trying to create some cognitive conflict with three- and four-year-old children in a nursery in Morpeth, UK. I began by putting a builder's hat on one of the girls and asking what her name would be, to which they all replied 'Bob the Builder'. I then swapped the hat for a piece of paper with the name 'Bob' written on it and asked whether she was still Bob the Builder, to which they replied no. This led to the cognitive conflict of 'when I have a hat on my head, then I am Bob the Builder, but when I take the name Bob, then I am not Bob'.

If you watch the video, you will notice that I don't just ask the first question and leave it at that; I keep questioning and suggesting so as to create a sense of cognitive conflict in the children's minds. It is the same with the suggested activities here: make sure you question the children so that they get into the pit.

For example, if your children say the photograph of the play money is not real, then you can ask why not. They are likely to explain that it is 'toy' money. You can then say, 'Does that mean toys are not real?' They will say, 'Yes toys are real', which is contradictory to saying the play money is not real because it is a toy.

The method I am using here is what I called in my earlier books 'Wobblers'. I purposefully chose this term to evoke the sense of wobble experienced when learning to ride a bike, as described in Section 2.1. It is not about trying to belittle the children or make them feel stupid. Indeed, the opposite effect is intended: it is supposed to show respect by engaging in the children's ideas and exploring ideas together. In other words, it is about playing with ideas.

2.5.1 Wobblers

A great way to create cognitive conflict in the minds of your children is to use Wobblers. We have created a lot of different ones. The best for use with young children are shared here.

Wobbler one (if A = B)

This involves asking what something is, taking whatever your children say and then testing it by turning it around and adding a conflicting example. For instance:

Question: What is a friend? (This is A.)

Answer: Someone who is nice to me. (This is B.)

Question: So, if someone is nice to you (B), does that mean that someone who is nice to you is your friend (A)? For example, a stranger who says hello to you.

The process looks something like this:

If A = B, then does B = A?

A is the concept that you are considering, in this case 'friend'.

B is a child's response, in this case, 'Someone who is nice to me'.

Now add an example that will conflict with the definition: for example, 'a stranger who says hello' or 'the dentist who gives you a sticker for being brave'.

Note that you are not proving the children wrong by finding this counter-example. Instead, you are trying to find an example that will cause them to think a little bit more.

Here are some examples using the illustrations in Figure 10 (page 25):

You show the children two photographs: one of a dog and the other of a toy dog. You ask them which one is real. The sorts of answers your children might give and an idea about the questions you can respond with are as follows:

Photographs of a 'real' dog and a 'toy' dog

Children:	That one is real (pointing to the photograph of the dog).
You:	Why is that one real?
Children:	Because that one can bark.
You:	So, if something can bark, does that mean it is real? If I can bark, then does that make me real?
Children:	No. Real means you are really there.
You:	So, if something is really there, then does that mean it is real? For example, that other dog (pointing at the toy dog) looks like it is there too. And we are all here so we are all real, are we?
Children:	Yes. So both of those dogs are real.
You:	But they look so different from each other. Is that OK?
Children:	No. Because only that one (pointing at the 'real' dog) can bark, so that is the only one that is real.

Photographs of 'real' building and a LEGO building

You:	Which one is real?
Children:	They are both real
You:	How can they both be real? They both look so different from each other.
Children:	Because you can see them both.
You:	So, if you can see something, does that mean it is real? For example, everything in this room that we can see, is it all real?
Children:	Yes.
You:	So, if I see you dressed up as a king or queen, then are you a real king or queen.
Children:	No! We're just playing.
You:	So, does that mean you can't be real if you're just playing? For example, if we play a game together, then does that mean we would not be real?

Notice what we are doing: we are listening to the children's responses, then turning them around and adding an example. We are not proving they are wrong. Instead, we are trying to find reasons for them to think a bit more about the concept.

Looking back at the first example, suppose we had asked which one is real, they had said, 'The dog on the left' and we had said, 'Very good; well done!' How much thinking would have been required of the children? How much 'wobble' would have ensued? Very little! So, instead, we recommend that you use this phrase to capture the approach:

Wobblers do not prove anyone wrong. Instead, they create a sense of uncertainty that prompts children to think again.

Not all of our questions answered but all of our answers questioned

To examine the interaction a bit more closely, here is the first dialogue again, this time coded to show:

(A) The concept.

(B) The children's answer.

You: Why is that one real **(A)**?

Children: Because that one can bark **(B)**.

You: So, if something can bark **(B)**, does that mean it is real **(A)**? If I can bark **(B)**, then does that make me real **(A)**?

Children: No. Real **(A)** means you are really there **(B)**.

You: So, if something is really there **(B)**, then does that mean it is real **(A)**?

NOW TRY THIS

Think of the answers your children might give to the question, 'What is a friend?' For example, they might say, 'A friend is someone I play with' or 'A friend is someone I like'.

Write down six different answers that your children might say:

1

2

3

4

5

6

Now use this formula to think of examples you could use to create cognitive conflict in your children's minds:

If a friend (A) is . . . . (B),

Then does that mean . . . . (B) is a friend (A)?

For example, here's the first one for you:

If a friend (A) is someone I play with (B),

Then does that mean someone I play with (B) is a friend (A)?

For example, if a stranger joined us now and we all played a game together, would we all be friends?

Wobbler two (NOT A)

Another way to create wobble in your children's minds is to add a negative to 'If A = B'. Thus, the formula becomes:

If A = B, then if it's NOT B, is it also NOT A?

A is the thing you are considering, for example 'friend'.

B is a child's response, in this case, 'someone I play with'.

So this time, to create cognitive conflict, we ask:

- Does that mean if you do *not* play (not B) with your friend today that you are *not* friends (not A)?

Continuing the dialogue about the 'real' dog and the 'toy' dog:

Children:	No. Because only that one (pointing at the 'real' dog) can bark, so that is the only one that is real.
You:	So, if something can*not* bark, does that mean it is *not* real? For example, flowers can't bark, but they are real, aren't they?
Children:	Not plastic ones.
You:	What do you mean?
Children:	Plastic flowers aren't real
You:	So does that mean anything that is not plastic is real? For example, the toy dog is not plastic; it is made of fluffy cotton.

Notice the use of the formula:

Children:	No. Because only that one (pointing at the 'real' dog) can bark, so that is the only one that is real.
You:	So if something can*not* bark **(Not B)**, does that mean it is *not* real **(Not A)**? For example, flowers can't bark, but they are real, aren't they?
Children:	Not plastic ones.
You:	What do you mean?
Children:	Plastic flowers aren't real.
You:	So does that mean anything that is not plastic **(Not B)** is real **(A)**? For example, the toy dog is not plastic; it is made of fluffy cotton.

NOW TRY THIS

Look back at the answers you thought your children might give to the question, 'What is a friend'? This time, think of ways to create cognitive conflict in their minds by using the formula: If A = B, then if it's NOT B, is it also NOT A?

2.5.2 Comparisons

Comparing one concept with another is a good way to create thought-provoking wobble.

Another good way to create cognitive conflict in your young children's minds is to encourage them to compare two or more concepts. This technique is not so reliant upon dialogue, so you might find this works better with some of your less verbal children.

Examples of comparisons that work well with young children:

What is the difference between:

Thinking and dreaming?

Friends and best friends?

Playing and pretending?

Choosing and deciding?

Caring and kind?

Sad and lonely?

Family and friends?

Shape and size?

Animals and pets?

Houses and homes?

Secrets and lies?

Love and kindness?

Like and love?

Mind and brain?

This list shows a comparison between synonyms, but you could also go for a comparison of antonyms. For example:

Real and pretend

Brave and scared

Animals and people

Friends and strangers

Love and hate

Safe and dangerous

Happy and sad

Healthy and sickly

Telling lies and telling the truth

Pets and wild animals

Loud and quiet

Old and new

More and less

Hot and cold

2.5.3 Prepared questions

Over the next few pages, there are some recommended questions for creating wobble in the minds of young children.

Creating a set of prepared questions before you start a Learning Challenge activity with your children is a good way to begin, particularly if you are new to this approach. First of all, select a concept that you would like to explore with your children. Then think of some questions to start them off thinking. Here are some examples:

Being nice

- Should you always be nice?
- Is it always nice to let people play with you?
- What does being nice look like?
- Should we always be nice to everybody?

Being unwell

- What does it mean to be unwell?
- Can you become unwell just by thinking you are?
- Can you be healthy and still be unwell?
- Can sadness make you unwell?
- What can cause us to be unwell?

Colour

- What is your favourite colour?
- Why do we like some colours more than others?
- Why do we need colour?
- Do you dream and think in colour?
- What would the world be like without colour?
- What would it be like if colours were to swap around (e.g. grass is blue, oranges are purple)?
- Is colour real?
- How do colours make you feel?

Dreams

- Is dreaming the same as thinking?
- Do you have to be asleep to dream?
- Is it good to dream?
- Can you make yourself dream?
- Does everybody dream?
- What happens when you dream?

Friends

- What makes someone a good friend?
- What does a friend look like?
- Do you always have to be nice to your friends?
- If a friend won't share their sweets, does that mean they're no longer your friend?
- How do you know that someone is your friend?
- What do you need to do to be a friend?
- Could you build the perfect friend? What would they look like?

Heroes

- What is a hero?
- Do you have to be a good person to be a hero?
- Do heroes have to be tough and strong?
- Are all heroes brave?
- What is the difference between a hero and a superhero?
- Can anyone be a hero?

Home

- What is a home?
- What is the difference between a house and a home?
- Why do people live in different kinds of homes?
- What does a place need to have for it to be a home?
- Does everything need a home?
- What is special about your home?

Names

- Are names important?
- Do you like your name?
- If you had a different name, would *you* be different?
- Why do things need names?
- Do people or things look like their names?
- Do names have to be words?
- If everyone called you by a different name, what would your 'real' name be?

Pets

- What is a pet?
- Can anything be a pet?
- Can a person be a pet?
- Do pets have to be living things?
- What is the difference between a pet and a friend?
- What is good about having a pet?
- What is bad about having a pet?

Shape

- What is a shape?
- Does everything have a shape?
- How can something be shapeless?
- If you change the shape of something, does it become something else? (If a banana becomes the shape of a strawberry, is it no longer a banana?)
- Why is shape important?
- How many different shapes can you make with your body?

Telling lies

- What is a lie?
- What is the difference between a lie and a story?
- What's the difference between lying and not telling the truth?
- Can you tell lies without saying anything?
- Does everyone tell lies?
- Is it possible to never tell a lie?
- When might telling a lie be a good thing?

2.6 LEARNING CHALLENGE STAGE 3: CONSTRUCT UNDERSTANDING

After your children have been in the pit for a while, it is time for them to climb out. When we say 'after a while', we are being purposefully ambiguous about the timing. It might be that your children have gone into the pit and then the activity has stopped. That is OK! If your children

finish the session with more questions than when they started, that is a *good* sign. We shouldn't leave children in the pit every single time, but to do so some of the time is quite all right, so long as the whole activity has been run in a playful, good-natured way.

Normally, speaking with children between the ages of three and seven, it will take just ten to 15 minutes to get children into the pit. Then we will go off to do another activity, and then later, we will return to the activity to look at ways to climb out of the pit. This might be later the same day, or it might be later in the week.

In each of the activity ideas in Chapter 8, we have given suggestions for ways to help your children out of the pit. For now, here are some of our favourite methods. We call them 'Pit Tools'.

After your children have thought through some of the contradictions and wobbles they've encountered in the pit, you could help them to piece together better answers.

Over the next few pages, you will find lots of ways to help children clarify their thinking. This includes Concept Targets, Opinion Lines and Diamond Rankings.

2.6.1 Concept Targets

A Concept Target encourages children to think about how valuable an idea is compared to all the other ideas. The best ideas hit the 'target' by being placed bang in the middle. The good ideas that aren't quite the best are placed a bit further out. Then the weakest ideas are placed on the outside of the target. (See Figure 13.)

As with all early childhood activities, abstract ideas such as a 'Concept Target' can be made more 'real' with the right props. In this case, an outer hoop and an inner hoop on the floor might help.

2.6.2 Ranking

A good way to help your children sort through the many ideas they have come up with during the wobble phase is to rank those ideas. This can be done in a Linear Rank, a Diamond Rank, Pyramid Rank or any such shape that will prompt your children to think about the relative value of each answer.

Ranking helps children to pick out their favourite or best ideas.

Figure 13: Concept Target about friends

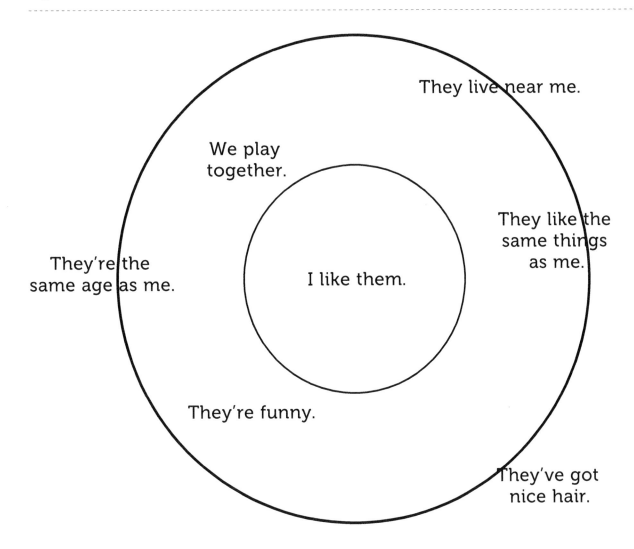

For each style of ranking shown, we have given two options: the introductory version and the more challenging version. We are assuming you will begin with whichever one you think best fits your children's stages of development.

Diamond Ranking

Start off with a diamond shape made up of four ideas, then progress onto a Diamond Nine when your children are ready.

A Diamond Rank begins with four cards and then progresses onto a full set of nine cards. The card placed at the top is considered to be the most important one; the next two cards below that are of equal importance to each other but less important than the top one. And so on. (See Figures 14 and 15.)

(Jill): Figure 16 shows the Diamond Ranks I created with a group of three- and four-year-olds recently. It came from an activity in which we were thinking about what makes a good superhero. During the week, we had read three books together: *Ladybug Girl* by Soman and Davis, *Wonder Woman* by Ralph Cosentino, and *The Mighty Thor* (Marvel Origin Story). We then thought about what each of the superheroes had in common with the others. The children came up with being brave, doing good things, being strong, being clever, wearing fancy dress, and helping others.

Figure 14: Introductory Diamond Rank

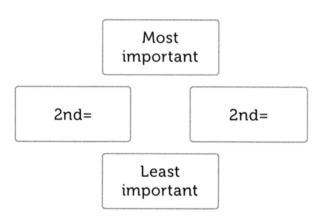

Figure 15: More challenging Diamond Rank

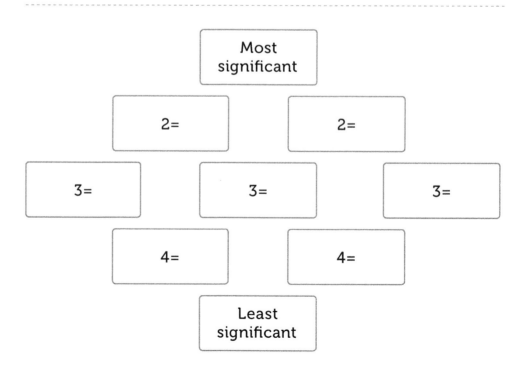

Figure 16: A Diamond Rank of superhero qualities

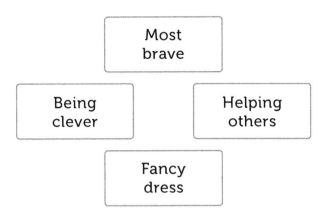

So we picked our favourite four ideas by taking a vote and then ranked them according to which we thought was the most important.

During the conversation, I kept questioning the children to cause a bit of wobble. Some examples are:

- Do superheroes have to wear fancy dress costumes?
- When the children said yes, I asked them: 'So when superheroes take their costumes off to have a bath, does that mean they are not superheroes anymore?'
- When we are brave, does that make *us* superheroes?
- Can you be a superhero if you don't help anybody?
- Can anyone be a superhero?

This first ranking activity lasted about 15 minutes, after which the children's concentration had pretty much evaporated! So, we returned to it later in the day to see whether we could add more of our ideas into the Diamond Rank. We didn't quite get to the point of adding nine cards into our rank, but we got pretty close, as you can see in Figure 17.

Figure 17: An almost complete Diamond Nine Rank

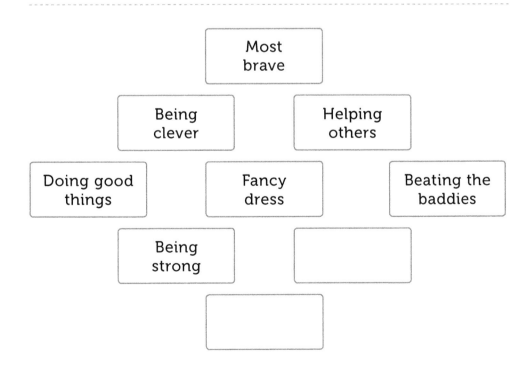

Figure 18: Introductory Pyramid Rank

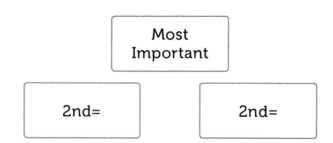

Figure 19: More challenging Pyramid Rank

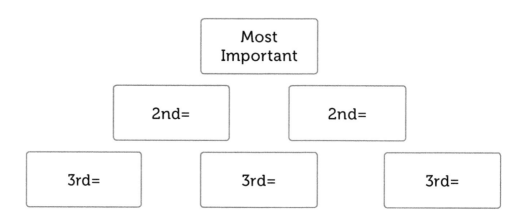

Pyramid Ranking

A Pyramid Rank begins with three cards and then can progress onto six or even ten if your children can handle so many possibilities at the same time. (See Figures 18 and 19.)

Line Ranking

A Line Rank is the most flexible style of ranking because it can include any number of variables. That said, it also means that your children can't say two or three factors are of the same value as they can in the Diamond and Pyramid Ranking. With Line Ranking, they have to give a different value to each idea. (See Figure 20.)

Figure 20: Line Rank

Figure 21: Venn Diagram involving three hoops

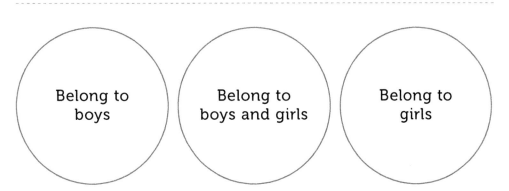

2.6.3 Venn Diagrams

Venn Diagrams are great visual tools for thinking, and they can work with children from about three years old onwards. Indeed, a great lesson we saw recently involved Venn Diagrams. The teacher asked her four-year-olds to sit in a circle, around which she placed 50 objects. She then showed them a picture of a four-year-old boy and asked them each to pick one of the objects that they thought belonged to the boy and to place it in a hoop that she laid on the floor alongside the boy's picture. As they did this, she asked them to give reasons why they thought, for example, the toothbrush that one of them had picked would belong to the boy.

Then she showed them a picture of a girl about the same age and asked them to do the same thing, only this time they were asked to place their chosen object into the hoop next to the girl's picture. The problem was that 30 children were in the class, and they had begun with 50 objects, 30 of which were already in the boy's hoop. So she asked the ten children who didn't have an object to think of a solution to their problem. Of course, they suggested moving some of the objects from the boy's hoop into the girl's hoop that they proceeded to do until the teacher asked the other children to challenge this if they so wished.

The children eventually decided that some objects could belong to boys and girls, at which point the teacher introduced a third hoop and laid it next to a picture showing a boy and a girl. (See Figure 21.) The activity finished with the children negotiating (by giving reasons, listening to one another and then making decisions) which objects should go in which hoop. Eventually, of course, all the objects ended up in the third hoop as the children realised they could all belong to boys *and* girls.

Of course, the normal way to draw a Venn Diagram is with overlapping circles, but for younger children, using three separate hoops works better, at least to begin with.

> Even Venn Diagrams can be used with young children so long as you begin with three separate hoops before progressing onto the standard two overlapping hoops.

2.6.4 Opinion Lines

Opinion Lines are very useful for beginning to explore statements using examples, gauging degrees of agreement and disagreement, or identifying degrees of preference. The best way to set up an Opinion Line is as follows:

1. Create a 'line' on the floor long enough for all your children to stand along. If you can mark this with a rope or some string, that would help.

2. Mark one end with an 'Agree' sign and the other with a 'Disagree' sign. Talk through the other descriptors shown in Figure 22 if you think your children are at the stage of development to understand *degrees* of agreement and disagreement.

3. Formulate a statement that expresses a point of view relating to the thinking activity your children are engaged in. Make sure the statement provokes different points of view. So don't give a statement such as 'It is nice to share' because all children have been instructed to believe that anyway! Instead, go for something like, 'We should *always* share with each other' because then that gives the possibility that some children will think, 'It is nice to share, but we don't *always* have to share'.

> Children love the physical nature of this activity. By moving themselves along the line, they can show their agreement or disagreement with an idea.

Figure 22: Opinion Line diagram

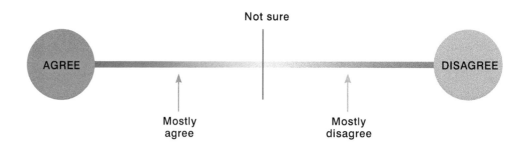

Here are some other examples:

- We always have to be friends with one another.
- Nobody should be left out.
- Pets are nicer than people.
- Every child should have a pet.
- Dogs are better than cats.
- We should take care of some animals more than others.
- Toys are only toys if you play with them.
- If you don't smile, then you should not be allowed to play games.
- Children should play all day long.
- It is always good to have a choice.
- Rules are there to be followed.
- If you can't see something, then it cannot be real.
- It is never right to tell lies.
- The older you get, the more you know.
- Grown-ups know best.
- Everybody grows a little bit every day.
- You should always eat your vegetables.
- It would be great to be happy all the time.
- We should all love one another.
- It is always good to learn new things.
- It is good to take risks.

4   Explain to your children that you are going to say something that they might agree with or they might disagree with. Say they will have time to think about it first, then you will ask them to stand on the part of the line that shows whether they agree, disagree or something in between.

5   Once your children have taken a place on the line, get them to give reasons as to why they have chosen to stand there. This could either be in pairs, or you could ask some of the children to explain their thinking to the whole group.

2.6.5 Opinion Corners

Opinion Corners can be used to show degrees of agreement or disagreement. They can also be used to help children pick from four completely different opinions.

Opinion Corners are really useful for giving your children four choices. These can either be agree a lot, agree a little, disagree a lot, disagree a little, or they could be four entirely different choices. For example, in Section 2.6.2, we shared the Diamond Ranking idea in which Jill asked her children to think about the qualities of a superhero. To help them make a decision about which is the most important quality, they could have voted by going to the corner that best represents their opinion. In that case, the Opinion Corner would look like Figure 23.

Figure 23: Opinion Corner about superheroes

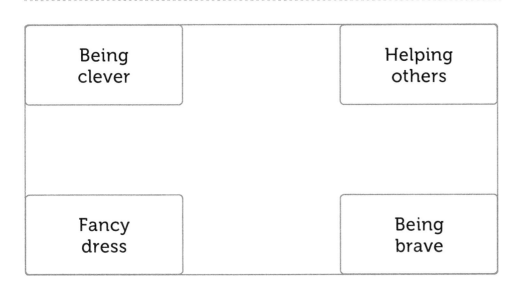

| Being clever | | Helping others |
| Fancy dress | | Being brave |

More typically, an Opinion Corner would have the four options shown in Figure 24.

Figure 24: Classic Opinion Corner

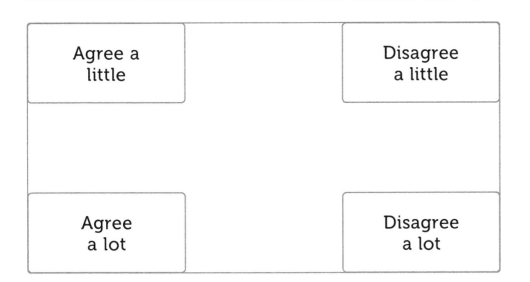

| Agree a little | | Disagree a little |
| Agree a lot | | Disagree a lot |

2.7 LEARNING CHALLENGE STAGE 4: CONSIDER THE LEARNING

The final stage of a Learning Challenge activity is for your children to think about what they have done so far and to think about how they could use their learning in other ways later on.

This would include asking such questions as:

1 What was the best idea you heard today?

2 What made you confused? What made you think?

3 What did you do when you were confused? What did you do when you were unsure/ puzzled?

4 What could we do next time to think even better than we did today?

If is often useful to think about each stage of the Learning Challenge in turn so that your children think back over the whole activity. This period of reflection does not have to happen

Once your children have climbed out of the pit, it is a good idea to encourage them to reflect on the thinking they have engaged in during the activity.

You could ask some of these questions at the end of the activity, or you could save them for later, depending on your children's concentration levels.

straightaway; it could, of course, come later if your children's concentration means they are ready for a break first.

Stage 1: Concept

When you get your children to think about the 'setting up' phase of a Learning Challenge activity, ask them one or more of these questions:

1   What did you like most about the story?

2   What do you think was the best idea (concept) we picked?

3   What was *your* best idea?

4   What was the most interesting question you heard someone ask? What was the best thing we wondered about?

5   What did you think the answer was first of all? What was your first answer/idea?

Stage 2: Conflict

Thinking about the cognitive conflict phase of the Learning Challenge activity, ask one or more of these questions:

1   What idea confused you/made you think the most?

2   As you started to wobble, how did that make you feel?

3   What else did you do when you were confused/unsure?

4   Do you think we thought of everything when we were in the pit?

5   How did you help others when you were in the pit?

Stage 3: Construct

Thinking about the constructing meaning phase of the Learning Challenge activity, ask one or more of these questions:

1   How did using the cards/objects/hoops (delete as appropriate) to talk about the idea help you to climb out of the pit?

2   Who helped you the most to climb out of the pit?

3   What was it that they said or did that helped you?

4   What was the best idea you had that helped others to climb out of the pit?

5   What did it feel like to climb out of the pit?

Stage 4: Consider

Thinking about the consider phase of the Learning Challenge activity, ask one or more of these questions:

1   If we did this again, what would you do the same?

2   If we did this again, what would you do differently?

3   Are you sure that we've got the right answer? Are you happy with the answer we came up with?

4   What do you think now compared to what you thought at the beginning of the activity? Is your answer/thinking different now from what it was at the beginning?

5   What questions do you still have about all of this? What are you still thinking/ wondering about?

6   What will you do next time we come together to do some super thinking?

As you will notice, the last set of questions is not just about looking back over the learning journey but also about looking forward to the next steps.

2.8 CHAPTER SUMMARY

This chapter has covered the following main points:

1   When children are given a choice about which activities they would like to have a go at, too many of them pick the easier option.

2   Children often pick the easier option because they want to be praised for getting things right.

3   When we teach children to ride a bicycle, we know they are going to wobble at first. When they do, we encourage them to keep going because we know that they are learning when they are wobbling. Yet too often, when children wobble with other activities, we rush to their aide to stop the wobble. This inadvertently stops the learning.

4   We should persuade children that challenging does not mean 'difficult'; it means 'interesting'.

5   *Challenging Early Learning* is about making early learning more 'interesting'.

6   The Learning Challenge is a well thought-out way to structure challenging activities for young children.

7   At the heart of a Learning Challenge activity is the 'pit'. This is another way of describing being out of your comfort zone.

NOW TRY THIS

Try this Learning Challenge with your colleagues so that you get a better sense of how it works in practice.

Stage 1: Choose a concept

Chosen concept: play

Create some questions about play. Here are some examples:

- **What is play?**
- **Is play always a good thing?**
- **Are children better at playing than adults are?**
- **Can play be challenging?**
- **Should play be challenging?**
- **Is this statement true? You don't stop playing because you grow old; you grow old because you stop playing.**
- **What is the difference between playing and having fun?**
- **Is playing always better than being serious?**
- **Is everything that children do in early childhood settings play?**
- **Is there more play in Early Years than at school? Why or why not?**
- **How do you know when you are playing?**
- **Can you be playing and not know you are?**

Stage 2: Create cognitive conflict

List six more answers to the question, what is play? The first two are given for you.

1   **Play is having fun.**

2   Play is pretending.

3   Play is . . .

4   Play is . . .

5   Play is . . .

6   Play is . . .

7   Play is . . .

8   Play is . . .

Using the Wobblers shown in Section 2.5.1, have a go in pairs creating cognitive wobble together. For example:

If play (A) is having fun (B), then if we have fun (B), does that mean it is play (A)? For example, if we have fun listening to a comedian, then is that play? Or if fun for us means skiing, then would we say skiing is play?

If play (A) is pretending (B), then if we are pretending (B), does that mean it is play (A)? For example, what if we pretend to be happy when we're actually feeling pretty miserable? Is that play?

If play (A) is . . . . (B), then if we . . . . (A), does that mean we are playing?.

Stage 3: Construct understanding

Use one of the Pit Tools shown in Section 2.6 to construct a better answer than the one you had at the beginning. Examples include:

1   Organise the ideas that you thought about at Stage 2 into a Line, Pyramid or Diamond Rank.

2   Or create a Venn Diagram to show the difference between play and work.

3   Or use the Concept Circle in Figure 25 to think of characteristics that would fall into the categories 'central to the concept', 'not sure' and 'not the concept'. We have placed some sample answers in already, but feel free to move them, of course!

Stage 4: Consider the learning journey

Here are some questions to think about at each stage of the Learning Challenge:

Stage 1: Concept

Thinking about the setting up phase of the Learning Challenge:

1   What was your first answer to the question, 'What is play?'?

2   How accurate did these early answers turn out to be?

3   How confident were you with your early answers?

4   What were the best questions you asked about play?

5   On reflection, would there have been a better question to ask?

6   How did your thinking affect your first steps in the learning journey?

Stage 2: Conflict

Thinking about the cognitive conflict phase of the Learning Challenge:

1   What was it about the concept or the question that led to cognitive conflict?

Figure 25: Concept Circle about play

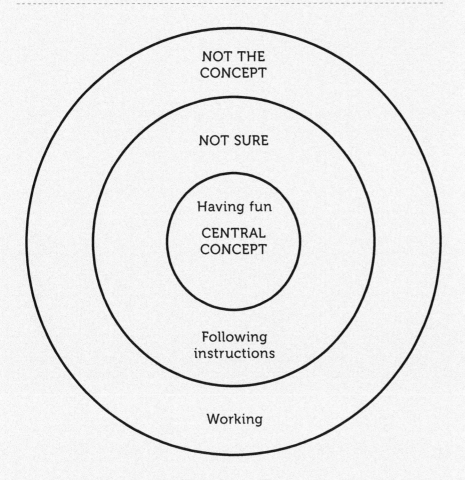

2   **Which two ideas formed the first cognitive conflict?**

3   **As you started to wobble, how did that make you feel?**

4   **How many examples of cognitive conflict did you create whilst you were in the pit?**

5   **Which two ideas conflicted the most and why?**

6   **Which ideas were dismissed easily and why?**

7   **Which questions did you (or somebody else) ask that helped to wobble even more?**

8   **Do you feel as if you examined *all* the options when you were in the pit?**

Stage 3: Construct

Thinking about the constructing meaning phase of the Learning Challenge:

1   **When did you start to make sense of all the conflicting ideas you had in the pit?**

2   **Which Pit Tool did you use to help you connect and explain your ideas?**

3   **Which was the most useful revelation you discovered?**

4   **How sure can you be that you did not accept easy answers?**

5   **What misunderstandings, misconceptions or assumptions did you uncover?**

6   If you had had time, what could you have done to improve your answer even further?

Stage 4: Consider

Thinking about the consider phase of the Learning Challenge:

1   In what ways do you understand the concept better now?

2   What would you do differently next time?

3   Which strategies did you use in this Learning Challenge that you could use with your children later?

4   What analogy, metaphor or example could you create to explain what you mean by play?

5   What advice would you give others about going through a Learning Challenge?

6   Which concepts do you think would be most suitable for thinking about with the children you work with?

Figure 26 presents the sorts of thoughts that often go through children's minds as they go through the Learning Challenge.

Figure 27 depicts our favourite illustration of the Learning Challenge because it shows seven clear steps that can be taken to help children really understand a concept.

Figure 26: Thinking through the Learning Challenge

Figure 27: Seven Steps to Understanding

3. DEVELOPING DIALOGUE WITH YOUNG CHILDREN

> YOU PROVIDE KIDS WITH GREAT STORIES AND TEACH THEM HOW TO USE THE TOOLS TO MAKE THEIR OWN.
>
> (Matt Groening, Emmy Award-winning cartoonist and creator of *The Simpsons*)

3.0 USING DIALOGUE TO DEVELOP CHILDREN'S LANGUAGE

By reading Chapter 2, you will have noticed that Learning Challenge activities rely a lot on dialogue among your children, as well as between your children and you.

Dialogue is one of the best vehicles for learning how to think, how to be reasonable, how to make moral decisions and how to understand another person's point of view. It is supremely flexible, instructional, collaborative and rigorous. At its very best, dialogue is one of the best ways for children to learn good habits of thinking.

At its best, dialogue is one of the best vehicles for teaching children good habits of thinking.

Dialogue also allows us as adults to intervene in the learning process by giving our children instant feedback, guidance and challenge.

Robin Alexander, a professor in the UK, is one of the main advocates for learning through dialogue, with many influential publications to his name. In one of his books, *Towards Dialogic Teaching: Rethinking Classroom Talk* (2006), he argues that:

1   Dialogue is undervalued in many schools and Early Years settings when compared with writing, reading and maths.

2   Dialogue does not get in the way of 'real' learning. In fact, by comparing PISA and other international tests, he shows it is possible to teach more through dialogue and yet still be 'at or near the top' of the tables.

Robin Alexander's research shows dialogue is not used as well as it might be with children.

3   Dialogue is the foundation of learning because it allows interaction and engagement with knowledge and with the ideas of others. Through dialogue, adults can most effectively intervene in the learning process by giving instant feedback, guidance and stimulation to learners.

Dialogue can give you a valuable insight into your children's beliefs, questions and misunderstandings.

4   Dialogue in education is a special kind of talk, in that it uses structured questioning to guide and prompt children's conceptual understanding.

Some of the other benefits of dialogue include the opportunity to ask appropriate questions, articulate problems and issues, imagine life's possibilities, see where things lead, evaluate alternatives, engage with one another and think collaboratively. A wide-scale improvement in such abilities would be no panacea, but can you think of many more significant educational achievements than these?

In the most basic sense, dialogue is the to and fro of talk between people who want to be understood. The moment a parent responds to their child's first sounds and engages them both in a communicative relationship, the foundations for dialogue are being built. Although it is similar to conversation, dialogue is also distinctly different. Whereas a conversation might go nowhere (or indeed anywhere), a dialogue properly defined and conducted, always goes *some*where (for example, answering an important question or making a decision together).

Dialogue is different from 'conversation'. Conversation can go 'anywhere', whereas dialogue always has a forward motion towards an agreed 'somewhere'.

Dialogue is not the Initiate-Response-Evaluate (IRE) model of questioning that is used in so many interactions between adult and child. Though this style of questioning does have some place in education, it is really only a way of checking children's factual recall. The Initiate step very often begins with an adult's question; for example, 'What are the three primary colours?' This is followed by a Response from a child; for example, 'Red, blue, yellow'. The adult then Evaluates this response and either confirms or corrects; for example, 'Well done, that's right!' Of course, there is nothing particularly wrong with this approach, but it tends not to challenge children beyond their first answer, whereas dialogue seeks to encourage children to go much further in their thinking and use of language.

Dialogue is a combination of conversation and inquiry.

The best way to think about dialogue is that it is conversation *and* inquiry. Dialogue combines the sociability of conversation with the skills of framing questions and constructing answers.

Dialogue is about working collaboratively to understand what has not yet been understood and to form reasoned opinions and further questions. The IRE structure is compatible with dialogue, but it is not the same as dialogue. Dialogue can take participants further. It can help your children to become capable thinkers, willing and able to learn, reason and express themselves clearly and confidently. At its best, dialogue will also foster encouragement, engagement, understanding and exploration.

Graham Nuthall research shows that adults are unaware of very many of the interactions between children. Dialogue can help to open up this world.

Professor Graham Nuthall spent years recording and evaluating dialogue by putting microphones on children and recording everything they said. He used this approach because his early research had led him to conclude that up to 40% of what happened amongst children was missed by adults.

Nuthall shared his findings in *The Hidden Lives of Learners* (2007). In it, Nuthall stated that:

1   Children live in a personal and social world of their own.

2   Children already know at least 40% of what adults have planned for them to learn.

3   A third of what each child learns is not learnt by any other child in the room.

4   Children learn how and when the adults will notice them and how to give the appearance of active involvement.

5   A quarter of the specific concepts and principles that children learn are critically dependent on private talk amongst themselves.

These five points in themselves are a strong justification for increasing the quantity and quality of dialogue in education.

Dialogue can give adults precious insights into the lives of their children.

Dialogue should help us as adults to understand the personal and social world of children; it should give us a better insight into what our children already know so that we can plan activities more accurately; it can provide a better opportunity for children to share with each other their own and often unique insights; it should cause children to be less concerned about *pretending* to be actively involved and actually help them to *be* engaged; and it should continue to help children to process and understand concepts and ideas – only this time it will be to the benefit of many others in the group and not just to the children's closest friends.

It is often the case that when we use dialogue really well with our children, we find out far more about them than we would normally. In dialogue, children reveal their likes and dislikes, their questions and their assumptions, their worries and their aspirations.

Dialogue is a supremely flexible and stimulating instrument of thought. As children get older, the issues they need to understand, the judgements they need to make and the relationships they need to maintain become more complex. The turn-taking structure of dialogue that leads a child to learn the rudiments of language also serves as a means of thinking about complex issues. Thus, dialogue is holistic in its intentions and its outcomes.

3.1 DIFFERENT TYPES OF TALK

Neil Mercer found three main types of talk amongst children: cumulative, disputational and exploratory. Of these, Mercer identifies exploratory talk as the type most like to support children's learning.

Neil Mercer described three types of talk that typically happen in both Early Years settings and schools: cumulative talk, disputational talk and exploratory talk. Of these three, Mercer identified exploratory talk as the most powerful for learning. He explains exploratory talk as:

> that in which partners engage critically but constructively with each other's ideas. Relevant information is offered for joint consideration. Proposals may be challenged and counter-challenged but if so, reasons are given and alternatives are offered. Agreement

is sought as a basis for joint progress. Knowledge is made publicly accountable and reasoning is visible in the talk.

(Mercer, 2000, p. 98)

Consider the key phrases in the Mercer quote that refer to powerful learning: 'joint consideration', 'counter-challenge', 'reasoning', 'alternatives offered', 'agreement', 'joint progress'. All of these are fundamentally related to an ethos in which learning takes place through dialogue and in which children are not only challenged but expect to be challenged.

However, when Rupert Wegerif (2002) looked into the types of talk found in classrooms, he discovered that very little exploratory talk occurs when children work together in groups. Instead the less learning-focussed types of talk predominate, and children more naturally lean towards disputational or cumulative talk.

> However, Rupert Wegerif found that very little exploratory talk takes place between children unless children are taught how to.

Before we look at how to best develop and use exploratory talk with your children, let's examine what these other two types are.

3.2 CUMULATIVE TALK

This type of talk is typically heard when friendship groups work together or when unfamiliar group members are getting to know one another. The talk is positive and affirming, making everyone feel included and welcome. The participants rarely criticise one another or the ideas being put forward. Not everyone in the group takes part, nor is everyone expected to. The group accepts first ideas and does not try to go beyond these. This leads to an accumulation of 'common knowledge' and a sense of 'harmony in the group'.

> Cumulative talk is positive and affirming but uncritical and too easy-going.

Cumulative talk is characterised by repetitions, confirmations and elaborations.

Here is an example from a group of four-year-olds who were playing in the sand pit:

Child 1:	Let's build a castle here.
Child 2:	OK. I'll dig it.
Child 3:	I'll dig this bit then.
Child 2:	OK, you do that and I'll do this.
Child 4:	(Nods)
Child 1:	I like this castle.
All:	Me too.

Cumulative talk such as this dialogue might seem good. The children had developed a positive atmosphere and were playing together nicely. The downside is that there was no challenge. The children did not wobble at all. The first child made a suggestion, and they all went along with it. No consideration was given to what else they could do. No one suggested an alternative place for the castle or even an additional feature such as a house next door. They group got on and built the castle without much fuss but also without very much challenge or dialogue.

NOW TRY THIS

Listen for examples of cumulative talk in your setting. Share some examples with your colleagues, and think through these questions together:

1   **How often does cumulative talk take place amongst our children?**

2   **What are the positive elements of this type of talk?**

3   **What are the drawbacks to it?**

4   **Are there particular children who spend most of their time engaging in cumulative talk?**

5   **What could we do to encourage these children to challenge one another a bit more?**

3.3 DISPUTATIONAL TALK

Disputational talk is competitive and often critical for the sake of being critical.

This type of talk is much more negative than cumulative talk. Disputational talk is critical of individuals (and their ideas), focuses on differences, is competitive and is all about being seen to 'win'. When engaged in disputational talk, children do not work together very well. Individuals within the group dominate. Mistakes are criticised and perhaps even ridiculed.

Disputational talk is characterised by short interactions, there is little attempt to listen to one another and the talk is dominated by opinions and counter-opinions.

Here is an example from a group of four- and five-year-olds who were building models with LEGOs:

Child 1:	What are you doing?
Child 2:	It is a tower.
Child 1:	It looks silly.
Child 2:	So? It's better than yours.
Child 3:	You're doing it wrong. It's going to break.
Child 2:	So what? I'll do it again.
	(The LEGO tower collapses.)
Child 3:	Told you.
Child 2:	I'm going to build another one, and you can't help.
Child 4:	Can I help?
Child 2:	No.
Child 2:	I'm doing this, and it's going to be the best one.

Although this might seem as if the children were fighting over the LEGOs, they weren't. In fact, they were engaging with each other about the task, but they were doing so in a negative manner. Although child one was actually trying to give advice, what he said sounded like criticism of the second child.

NOW TRY THIS

Listen for examples of disputational talk amongst your children. Share some examples with your colleagues, and think through these questions together:

1. **How often does disputational talk take place amongst our children?**

2. **Is there anything positive about it at all?**

3. **Are there particular children who spend most of their engaging in disputational talk?**

4. **What could we do to encourage these children to challenge one another in a more positive, supportive manner?**

5. **Do personality clashes affect the likelihood of disputational talk taking place?**

3.4 EXPLORATORY TALK

Exploratory talk is characterised by longer exchanges, use of questions, reflection, explanation and speculation. It should make full use of critical thinking as well as being very creative. That is what makes it so powerful for learning and language development.

Exploratory talk is full of reflections, wondering, encouragement and challenge.

To make best use of the approach, your children should explore ideas in an open-minded manner. They should expect to be challenged by you and by other children. Any questions or suggestions they make should be done in a respectful and thoughtful way. There should be no embarrassment if they get it 'wrong' because it is all about exploration and inquiry.

Achieve this type of talk amongst your children, and the results can be very impressive.

Wegerif and Scrimshaw (1997) studied the impact of teaching primary school children how to engage in exploratory talk. They found that after five weeks of using exploratory talk, the number of questions that children asked one another increased from 17 to 86; the number of reasons given more than doubled; and the number of speculations (what if . . . ?) rose from two to 35. In total, the number of words used by the children almost doubled.

They concluded that the explicit teaching of exploratory talk led to an improvement in the quality and variety of language used by children, as well as an improvement in the active participation by children in group activities. This suggested a strong connection between social interaction (thinking together) and improved cognitive development.

Here is an example of exploratory talk that Jill recently ran with a group of four-year-olds:

Jill:	Who has a favourite toy?
Child 1:	My best toy is my dinosaurs.
Child 2:	My Freddy teddy is my favourite. I sleep with him every night and cuddle and kiss him.
Child 3:	I like all my toys. They are all my favourites.
Child 4:	My scooter is best because it is blue and goes really fast.
Jill:	Is your favourite toy always the best toy you have?
Child 4:	Yes, it is the best because it goes really, really fast.
Jill:	So, do the best toys go really fast then?
	(Child 1, 3 and 4 nod in agreement.)
Jill:	How about Freddy teddy? Is he fast?
Child 4:	No, teddies don't do anything.
Child 2:	Freddy teddy does. He does lots of things.
Child 1:	Like what?
Child 2:	He can play games and he can talk. And he sleeps in my bed.
Child 3:	Can he really talk?
Child 2:	Yes, you just press the button and he says things.
Child 3:	So, is he your favourite then?
Child 2:	Yes. He is the best.
Jill:	There is that word, 'best' again. Is that the same as 'favourite'? Are your favourite toys always your best toys?
Child 5:	Don't know. My favourite toy is my football, but it's not a very good one.

If you compare this dialogue with the examples of cumulative and disputational talk, you should notice the following differences:

1   Reasons are now offered.

2   Explanations are longer.

3   Children ask questions of one another.

4   Children suggest possible answers for one another.

5   The children are listening to one another.

6   They are all expressing their ideas.

7   It is collaborative rather than competitive.

8   Although they haven't made a decision (yet), they are nonetheless moving towards a consensus.

NOW TRY THIS

Listen for examples of exploratory talk amongst your children. Share some examples with your colleagues, and think through these questions together:

1   **How often does exploratory talk take place amongst your children?**

2   **Are there particular children who are better able at engaging in exploratory talk than others?**

3   **What could we do to support children to engage in exploratory talk more often?**

4   **What could we call exploratory talk so that our children know what type of talk we are trying to get them to engage in?**

5   **What kind of talk have you and your colleagues been engaging in whilst talking about these different types of talk?**

3.5 ENCOURAGING EXPLORATORY TALK

Agreeing on a set of supportive and encouraging ground rules can help to prepare for exploratory talk.

Exploratory talk occurs in an environment in which children feel comfortable to explore ideas with one another. They will need to trust one another and know that questions and challenges help their thinking rather than criticise or make fun of them.

Having a set of ground rules can help to set the right tone. The following list could be used if you like:

• We share our ideas and listen to one another.

• We talk one at a time.

• We respect each other's opinions.

• We say why we think what we think.

• We ask each other 'why?'

• We try to agree in the end if we can.

These ground rules are not set in stone! You do not have to use all of them or even some of them. Indeed, it might be better to create a set of rules with your children so that they have more understanding of them and ownership over them.

Whichever way you decide to go – presenting the preceding list or creating a new list with your children – make sure you talk about the behaviours associated with each ground rule. Share the list with the children and with their parents. Display them prominently in a classroom or Early

Years setting. Of course, the children might not be able to read them yet, but displaying them helps to remind you and your colleagues what they are!

As well as a set of ground rules for your children, it is important to model the following attitudes and beliefs:

If you model attitudes such as respect, interest and curiosity, then exploratory talk is more likely to flourish.

- I am interested in and respect your ideas.

- I will show my interest by listening to you and questioning you.

- I am confident you are the sort of person who can come up with interesting questions, opinions, reasons and examples.

- I will think about your questions, interests and ideas as much as I can.

- I am creating a thinking environment where we can all engage in questions together and work towards the best answers and understandings.

- We should all feel secure enough to take intellectual risks.

If you look back at the video online that we suggested earlier (youtu.be/jZ4iNeNtLOM), you will see James trying to show these dispositions. In fact, if you watch it again, you should also notice that James gives no praise to the children. That is not because he was being unnecessarily harsh but because he felt that by showing that he was interested in their ideas, that he was confident in their abilities to engage with the questions, that he was creating an environment in which it was safe to explore all ideas, and that actually there was no need for praise. The atmosphere was supportive enough as it was without the need for praise as well.

For another explanation of how you can help your children develop exploratory talk, we encourage you to read Section 6.2, example 3.5.

3.6 REPEATING, REFLECTING, REPHRASING AND EXTENDING

There are many ways to encourage children to think and talk more. Here are a few that can really help younger children.

Techniques such as repeating, reflecting, rephrasing and extending can help children engage in exploratory talk.

Repeating: When a child says something, invite other children to repeat word for word what they said. So, if a three-year-old said, 'My favourite colour is red', then we can ask the other children in the group to repeat this by saying:

> Annabel says, 'My favourite colour is red'.

Reflecting: This time, when a child says something, invite other children to reflect what they said. This means the listeners say what the first child said but put it in such a way as to speak on their behalf. For example:

> Annabel's favourite colour is red.

Rephrasing: When a child says something, invite other children to rephrase what they said. They should keep the meaning but use different words. For example:

> The colour that Annabel likes most is red.

Extending: Extending is when you invite a child to reflect *and* add to what another child has said. For example:

> Annabel says that her favourite colour is red. So I think she doesn't like the other colours in that picture as much.

Encouraging your children to extend what others have said requires much more skill than the others do. This is one of the many reasons why it is so worthwhile. Others include the fact that it tends to get your children out of their comfort zone; it encourages them to extend their language; it helps them to show respect by adding to what another person has said; and it gives them the opportunity to test their understanding of what someone else has said.

When your children begin using the extending strategy, it is a very good idea to check with the original child whether the extension was correct. Here is an example James observed in a nursery recently. The children were five years old.

Thomas:	I have got three guinea pigs, a dog and a cat.
Marianne:	That's a lot of pets.
Ben:	Thomas must really like animals.
Helen:	I wonder if he likes all animals.
Teacher:	That is a great question, Helen. Before we go any further, can we ask Thomas if Ben was right to say, 'He must really like animals'?
Thomas:	Yes, I do.
Helen:	But do you like all animals?
Thomas:	Yes.
Teacher:	Can anyone think of examples of animals that Thomas might not like?
Sarah:	I don't think he likes rats. Or snakes.
Lucy:	Or lizards.
Teacher:	So, Thomas. Lots of people are trying to guess what you think. Can you tell us which ideas are right?
Thomas:	I've got a pet rat.
Helen:	Ah, so he likes rats then!
Thomas:	But I don't like snakes.
Elisabeth:	Maybe that's because snakes eat rats.
Teacher:	What a clever connection to make, Elisabeth. Thomas, is Elisabeth right?
Thomas:	I don't know. I guess.

NOW TRY THIS

It seems to us that there are six instances of the children extending what Thomas said and two examples of reflecting. Do you agree? Can you point them all out?

We have shown our coding in the Appendix.

3.7 CHAPTER SUMMARY

This chapter has covered the following main points:

1 Dialogue is one of the best vehicles for teaching children how to think.

2 Dialogue combines the sociability of conversation with the skills of framing questions and constructing answers.

3 Dialogue helps adults understand the personal and social world of children and gives a better insight into what they are thinking.

4   Neil Mercer (2000) found three main types of talk in educational settings: cumulative, disputational and exploratory.

5   Cumulative talk is too easy-going and nice; disputational talk is too negative; exploratory is just right because it challenges, engages and extends children's thinking and language.

6   Ground rules for talk can help to set the right tone for learning.

7   We can extend children's thinking and language by encouraging children to repeat, reflect, rephrase and extend what others have said.

4. ENGAGING CHILDREN'S THINKING SKILLS

4.0 LEARNING HOW TO THINK

This chapter focuses on teaching children *how* to think. It is not about *what* to think but about *how* to think. Before we dive in, let's start with a story.

Teaching children *how* to think should be a key part of education.

Many years ago, we (the authors) attended an international conference in Bulgaria. The focus was Philosophy for Children. In addition to the 200 delegates from around the world, the organisers also invited some local teenagers to take part in proceedings. Midway through the four-day event, James was asked to facilitate a community of inquiry with these teenagers for the other delegates to observe.

He began the session with a fictional story about two hunters, Hank and Frank, who are chased by a talking bear. The teenagers then created a number of philosophical questions from which they chose their favourite: 'Why sacrifice yourself for others?' After a short pause for quiet reflection, James invited an eager young man to start us off by giving his first thoughts. This is what he said:

> It seems to me that 'sacrifice' is the most important concept in this question. I think someone might sacrifice themselves based on instinct, impulse or intuition. Of course, two of these are in the cognitive domain and one is in the affective domain, so I suppose we need to determine which of these is more likely in any given situation before we can answer the question effectively.

All the other delegates were nodding approvingly at the boy's apparent confidence in thinking about and analysing the concept of sacrifice. James, on the other hand, was like a rabbit caught in the headlights; he certainly had not been expecting that response!

To grab some thinking time for himself, he asked the teenagers to decide what these terms – 'instinct', 'impulse' and 'intuition' – had in common. Whilst they did that, James asked a friendly philosopher to suggest what to do next.

Reconvening, James asked one girl to give her group's answer. She will forevermore be James's favourite because she replied: 'Instinct, Impulse and Intuition have one thing in common . . . they are all names of perfumes'. (At last: a 'normal' teenager!)

Once the hour-long discussion had finished, James made a beeline for the organisers and moaned that they had staged all this: 'You could've told me you'd invited only the most talented philosophers from across Bulgaria to join us!' he said. They laughingly explained they had simply invited volunteers from the local area to take part – there had been no selection process.

'So how come they're so adept at thinking?' James inquired. 'Because they've been taught how to think from an early age', they said. 'But so have children in the UK and yet we haven't come across young teenagers as skilled in thinking as your students', James countered. Their response was something that initially vexed, then intrigued and ultimately emboldened us both: 'From what we've seen in Western countries, you don't seem to teach children *how* to think; instead you only teach them *what* to think'.

The more we work in Early Years settings and schools around the world, the more we think these Bulgarian teachers may have been right.

For example, ask children at the end of primary school (9- to 11-year-olds) if they think stealing is wrong, and they will all answer yes. But if they are asked why Robin Hood is thought of as a good man if stealing is wrong, they will retort, 'Because he robbed from the rich and gave to the poor'. Perhaps there's nothing too controversial there, but if you press them to decide whether it would be OK to steal, let's say from a bank, and give the proceeds to poor people, they almost always say yes. Rarely do the children seem troubled by the fact that stealing from anybody, no matter what the funds are used for, is against the law.

This suggests the Bulgarian teachers might be right – that too many children are being taught what, rather than how, to think?

Yet teaching children *how* to think feels like something of an abstract concept. Perhaps the simplest way to picture it is to consider one strategy for thinking that we all use when faced with a difficult choice, to list advantages and disadvantages. Creating this structure in our head is common to all of us. But it is not a structure we were born with – we were taught it, and it has become one of our 'thinking tools'. Dialogue allows us to model structures for thinking, for example, by asking questions, giving counter-examples, asking for reasons, justifying answers, adding to the last idea you heard. All of these are new thinking structures, and you are explicitly modelling and teaching them with the children.

In another example, we often notice teachers and parents praising children for saying the 'right' thing: 'it is wrong to kill', 'we must always be nice', 'you should never lie', and so on. And on the face of it, this might seem reasonable. After all, we want children to be moral and to do the right thing. However, what happens when they are faced with a dilemma but, up to that point, have only ever followed instructions? Such dilemmas might include eating meat whilst maintaining that killing is wrong; always telling the truth even if it is likely to hurt someone; always being nice even to someone who is either being racist or bullying a friend. What then?

Many parents will reply that they trust their children to do the right thing. But how do children know what the 'right' thing is unless they have learnt how to make moral decisions for themselves? In other words, how can they be moral if they haven't learnt how to think or haven't developed at least some wisdom?

To answer this, it is important to distinguish between types of thinking that, to our minds, consist of two main categories: routine and reflective.

> **Routine thinking** includes the thinking we do almost subconsciously when, for example, riding a bike, walking or quoting our telephone number.

> **Reflective thinking** includes thinking about the consequences of our actions and deciding on the relative importance of factors affecting our decisions about what to think or do.

If a child learns to speak or write fluently but then does so thoughtlessly or inconsiderately, he is likely to upset others. If she memorises lots of facts but doesn't learn how to use them wisely, then her knowledge will be limited in its application. Therefore, the development of thinking includes the ability and willingness to exercise the right type of thinking at the right time for the right purpose. That is exactly what teaching children how to think can improve!

The sorts of thinking skills we should aim to teach young (and old) children are shown in Figure 28. This is not an exhaustive list. It should also be adapted to suit the developmental stage of the children you are working with.

Teaching children how to think includes improving the ways in which they process information, ask questions, give reasons, look for counter-examples and so on.

Teaching children how to think focuses particularly on improving their reflective thinking.

Teaching children how to think will always work best when done in conjunction with these values.

NOW TRY THIS

A good starting point for using the list of thinking skills shown in Figure 28 is to choose three that you think your children are ready for and would benefit most from. Then plan with your colleagues some ways you can help your children practise these skills. This shouldn't happen in isolation, of course. Promote positive interactions with children by:

- **Listening attentively.**

- **Being sensitive to different children's needs.**

- **Modelling good thinking.**

- **Using questioning techniques to promote wonder (see Chapter 5 for ideas).**

- **Encouraging children to ask questions.**

- **Supporting children to think collaboratively.**

- **Giving children time to talk.**

- **Giving children space to think (see Section 5.2).**

Promote opportunities for imagination and creative play by:

- Modelling open-mindedness.
- Focussing more on the process of thinking than on getting the 'right' answer.
- Emphasising the open-endedness of thinking tasks.
- Offering alternatives.
- Creating ambiguity.
- Welcoming ideas even if you don't understand the relevance of them.

Enable reflection and metacognition by:

- Encouraging children to think about what they are doing.
- Asking children to think about alternative ways to do things.
- Welcoming commentary.
- Promoting dialogue and questioning.
- Building on previous thinking.

Figure 28: Important thinking skills for young children

Here are some of the skills of thinking that you could help your young children develop.

Anticipate	Elaborate	Rank
Apply	Estimate	Represent
Cause	Evaluate	Respond
Choose	Explain	Say why
Classify	Give examples	Select
Compare	Give reasons	Sequence
Connect	Group	Show how
Contrast	Identify	Solve
Decide	Organise	Sort
Describe	Predict	Summarise
Discuss	Question	What if

In the next section, we share some thinking activities that you might want to try with your children. Whichever ones you use, think about the thinking skills that you could promote during the activity.

In the games that follow, please note:

1 We have highlighted the main thinking skills involved, but other skills could easily be developed alongside them.

2 Although there is no right or wrong answer, there are probably better ones in each case. To help identify the higher-quality responses, encourage your children to give reasons and to compare the relative merits of each answer they come up with.

The rest of this chapter describes some of the games you can play with young children to help them develop their skills of thinking.

4.1 TRANSPORTER

Main thinking skills:

- Predict outcomes.
- Look for alternatives and possibilities.
- Think flexibly.
- Ask, 'What if?'

Activity

Place an object on a chair such as a teddy bear or doll's house. Your children should try to move the object to the floor without touching it or the chair. The object has to land safely on the floor without being damaged. If you want to make things a bit easier, then you could provide some objects to help them such as a skipping rope, some large pieces of card or some drumsticks. Or you could let the children go on a scavenger hunt for suitable objects.

4.2 ODD ONE OUT

Main thinking skills:

- Find relevant information.
- Compare and contrast.
- Make connections.
- Give reasons.

Activity

Show your children three objects, and ask them which is the 'odd one out' and why. You are looking for a whole range of answers, not just the obvious ones. Figures 29, 30, 31 and 32 give you some examples, but you can use any three objects, sounds, images and the like.

Sample answers from four-year-olds:

The giraffe is the odd one out because the other two have paws.

The dog is the odd one out because it is the only one that barks.

The cat is the odd one out because cats make me sneeze (and the other two do not).

Sample answers from five-year-olds:

1 is the odd one out because the other two have got curly parts on them.

6 is the odd one out because it is the age that I will be soon (and the other two are not).

10 is the odd one out because it is the only one with two digits.

Figure 29: Odd One Out with a cat, a dog and a giraffe

Figure 30: Odd One Out with numbers

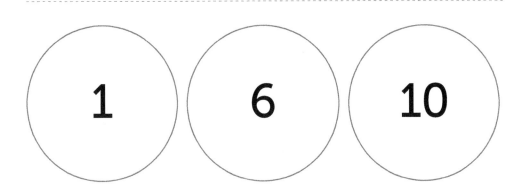

Sample answers from three-year-olds:

> The big sock is the odd one out because it is black (and the other two are not).
>
> The tights are the odd one out because they are for two feet (and the other two are not).
>
> The little sock is the odd one out because it has pink on it (and the other two do not).

Sample answers from four- and five-year-olds:

> The recorder is the odd one out because it is the only one you blow.
>
> The drum is the odd one out because it is the only one you hit with a stick.
>
> The tambourine is the odd one out because you shake it (and you don't shake the other two).

Figure 31: Odd One Out with socks

Figure 32: Odd One Out with musical instruments

4.3 THAT IS WHAT I WAS THINKING

Main thinking skills:

- Make connections.
- Give reasons.
- Look for alternatives and possibilities.
- Think flexibly.

Activity

Child A says what they were thinking of. Child B says what they were thinking of. Child A should then try to make enough links to suggest that they were both in fact thinking of the same thing.

Example: Child A says 'cat'; Child B says 'banana'. Child A then says: 'That's what I was thinking about because my cat was playing with a banana trying to get it open'.

4.4 THE THREE WHYS (MEN)

Main thinking skills:

- Give reasons.
- Think flexibly.
- Use precise language.
- Identify improvements.

Activity

Ask at least three successive questions that begin with 'why'. You can see an example of this in the video previously mentioned in which James is working with some three- and four-year-olds in Morpeth, UK (youtu.be/jZ4iNeNtLOM). In that video, the 'why' questions are as follows:

James:	If I put this builder's hat on your head then you become Bob the Builder; but if I put this name badge that belongs to Daniel next to you, do you become Daniel?
Ava:	No.
James:	Why not? (first why)
Ava:	Because it's silly.
James:	Why is it silly? (second why)
Ava:	Because it feels funny.
James:	Why does it feel funny? (third why)
Ava:	Because my name is Ava. I don't want to be called Daniel because that's not my real name.

The aim of three questions beginning with 'why' is to tease out more thinking and reasoning from your children than might normally be heard.

4.5 A REASONABLE HOLIDAY

Main thinking skills:

- Make connections.
- Infer and deduce.
- Seek further details.
- Develop criteria.

Activity

Show a suitcase full of objects to your children. Invent an imaginary character, and tell the children that the suitcase belongs to him/her. Invite your children to take turns selecting an object from the suitcase and to say whether it would be good to take that object on holiday or not.

Example objects include book, brush, mirror, cuddly toy, dice, pen, shorts, hat, sunglasses, banana, screwed-up paper, plastic flower, drumstick, boiled sweets, mobile phone, money, plastic farm animals, a plastic bag, swimming goggles and so on.

As the children engage in this activity, they should very soon realise that they don't have enough information. So, all being well, they will begin to ask questions such as:

Where is the character going on holiday?

Is it going to be warm/cold/wet/dry etc.?

Is the owner an adult or a child?

How long are the owner going for?

When your children start asking these sorts of questions, then take time to celebrate the question rather than going immediately to answering them. For example, you could say: 'What a great question. Can anyone else think of a question they would like to ask? Are there any questions that we already know the answer to?'

4.6 WHAT IF?

Main thinking skills:

- Identify problems.
- Think flexibly.
- Look for alternatives and possibilities.
- Search for value.

Young children love this game because it gives them the opportunity to let their imaginations run away with them. Ask them any number of 'What if . . . ?' questions, and see how they respond. For example:

What if . . .

- Horses were as small as guinea pigs?
- Rats could fly?
- Cucumbers were pink?
- Animals could read?
- Dreams were not allowed?
- Snakes could walk?
- Toys could talk?
- Dogs could be taught to drive?
- Rainbows could be climbed?
- Food cooked itself?
- Money grew on trees?
- All houses were made of gingerbread?
- Teeth cleaned themselves?
- Snow was warm?
- Vegetables tasted like chocolate?
- Everyone was always happy?
- Time went backwards?
- Humans could walk on water?
- Nobody ever told lies?
- Children made all the rules?
- Everyone looked the same?
- People never got old?

What would *you* do if . . . ?

A variation on the previous game is to ask your children what *they* would do if particular things were to happen. As with all the best early childhood games, encourage the other children to chip in with ideas or ask supplementary questions. For example:

What would *you* do if . . .

- You had no toys to play with?
- You were not allowed to talk for a whole day?
- We all had to swim to nursery?
- You could fly?
- You had a different name?
- You slept during the day and were awake all night?
- You were a king or queen?
- You couldn't use your legs?
- You could ride a unicorn whenever you wanted?
- You had to eat mud for breakfast?

4.7 STORYBOARDING

Main thinking skills:

- Think flexibly.
- Generate ideas.
- Give alternative suggestions.
- Identify improvements.

Activity

Divide your children into groups of about five and invite an adult to sit with each group. Ask the children a range of story prompt questions to help them create a story together. After each prompt is given, allow the children time to give their ideas and for the adult sitting with them to draw the children's responses on a large sheet of paper. Flip chart paper is perfect for this purpose.

Once you have asked the first question ('Who or what is the main character?'), give each group the chance to decide on their answer and then time for the adult to draw what the children told them. So, if one group decided on a 'girl', then the adult with that group should draw a cartoon girl on the flipchart paper. As you ask subsequent prompts, a cartoon storyboard will evolve in front of the children's eyes. They can then use this storyboard to retell their story to other children in the room.

Storyboard prompts:

1 Who or what is the main character? (For example, a boy, a girl, a horse or a piece of fruit?)

2 Describe the main character: what is she wearing and doing?

3 The main character is going on a journey: where is he going?

4 Who or what is with the main character?

5 Along the way, something bad happens: what is it?

6 Who or what comes to the rescue?

7 The rescuer is magical. What powers does he have?

8 Something happens that stops him using his magical powers: what is it?

9 The main character does something to help the rescuer: what does she do?

10 A very strange thing appears: what is it?

11 The main character has nearly arrived but what stands in her way?

12 How does your main character reach her journey's end, and how does she celebrate?

4.8 FORTUNATELY, UNFORTUNATELY

Main thinking skills:

- Generate ideas.

- Give suggestions.

- Make connections.

- Seek further details.

Activity

This storytelling activity alternates between fortunately and unfortunately. Sit with your children in a circle. Set the scene by beginning a story. Then invite the child sitting to your left to continue the story. They should start with 'Unfortunately, . . .'. If you are working with younger children, they could begin with 'But . . .', and the game will still work. Once the first child has given his idea, the child to his left continues the story. This time, she should begin with 'Fortunately . . .'.

The story continues, all the time alternating between fortunately and unfortunately. Here is an example from a group of five- and six-year-olds recently:

You:	Once upon a time, there was a horse called Sue.
Child 1:	But (unfortunately) . . . he didn't like being called Sue.
Child 2:	But (fortunately) . . . he was allowed to change his name to Harry.
Child 3:	But (unfortunately) . . . Harry was not a happy horse. He didn't like carrying people.
Child 4:	But (fortunately) . . . Harry was owned by Tina who was very small and very light.
Child 5:	But (unfortunately) . . . Tina's big fat brother jumped on top of Harry and hurt his back.
Child 6:	But (fortunately) . . . Harry was a strong horse and threw Tina's brother off his back and ran away.
Child 7:	But (unfortunately) . . . Harry met a dragon on the way.
Child 8:	But (fortunately) . . . the dragon was a friendly dragon who just wanted to be friends with Harry.
Child 9:	But (unfortunately) . . . every time the dragon opened her mouth, she would breathe fire at Harry.

NOW TRY THIS

Pick one of the games shown in this chapter to play with your children. Ask a friend or colleague to observe the activity so that afterwards the two of you can talk about what you observed and what thinking skills you thought the children were using. Also reflect on what could be done to improve or adapt the activity for different children.

4.9 CHAPTER SUMMARY

This chapter has covered the following main points:

1. We can help children learn *how* to think even better than they already do.

2. Routine thinking includes everything that we do almost subconsciously, for example, walking, sitting, breathing and dreaming.

3. Reflective thinking includes thinking about options and alternatives, consequences and assumptions, sorting and classifying and so on.

4. Teaching children how to think focusses primarily on improving reflective thinking.

5. There are many skills of thinking that we can help young children to develop and enhance; these include estimating, evaluating, giving reasons, connecting, organising, predicting, and questioning.

6. Thinking skills are never learnt in isolation; instead they are best learnt in an environment that promotes positive interactions and opportunities for imagination, creativity, reflection and metacognition.

7. There are eight thinking games in this chapter. All of them can be adapted to challenge or support, depending on the developmental stage of your children.

5. LISTENING, THINKING AND QUESTIONING

[KIDS] DON'T REMEMBER WHAT YOU TRY TO TEACH THEM. THEY REMEMBER WHAT YOU ARE.

(James Maury 'Jim' Henson, creator of the Muppets)

5.0 PATIENCE FOR LISTENING

For all the activities and recommendations in this book to work brilliantly, patience when listening to children is an absolute prerequisite. This was emphasised many years ago by Mary Budd Rowe (1986), who found that the average amount of time an adult waits after asking children a question before asking another question or giving a prompt is one second or less. That is not a lot of time for children, and it doesn't show much patience!

All children should be encouraged to wonder, elaborate and pause for thought. Budd Rowe suggested that a very simple way to make this more likely is by introducing 'wait time'. She observed that when adults wait for a minimum of 3 seconds *before* taking an answer from their children and then wait another 3 seconds *after* taking an answer, the effects can be staggering:

- The length of explanations amongst advantaged children increases fivefold and sevenfold amongst disadvantaged children.

- The number of volunteered, appropriate answers by larger numbers of children greatly increases.

- Failures to respond and 'I don't know' responses decrease from 30% to less than 5%.

- The number of questions asked by children rises.

- The academic scores of these children once they are in school showed a tendency to increase.

Budd Rowe's research is as relevant today as it was back then. And it is doubly pertinent to all the *Challenging Early Learning* activities recommended in this book because of their reliance on high-quality dialogue. It is also worth bearing in mind that Budd Rowe's research has been repeated many times over in many different countries since her work in the 1970s, and the results are consistent: in typical educational settings, children get very little time to process information, language and ideas and are therefore restricted in how well they can contribute to a dialogue.

There are also benefits for the adults running these activities if they wait longer. Robert Stahl (1990) noticed the following improvements when the wait time was increased to 3 seconds:

- Adults' questioning strategies tend to be more varied and flexible.

- Adults decrease the quantity and increase the quality (and variety) of their questions.

- Adults ask additional questions that require more complex information processing and higher-level thinking on the part of their children.

Incidentally, you can find out more about this research and some corresponding recommendations in *Challenging Learning Through Dialogue* (Nottingham, Nottingham, Renton, 2017).

A classic way to increase thinking time is through the use of the strategy Think-Pair-Share. This is a simple and yet effective way to give your children time to process their ideas and select the language needed to contribute to the dialogue. The convention typically follows these steps:

- Someone asks a question.

- Children **think** to themselves for a minimum of 3 seconds.

Mary Budd Rowe's research showed that the typical 'wait time' between an adult asking a question and either a child answering or the adult continuing to talk is just 0.8 second!

There are many advantages for children when the 'wait time' between question and response is increased to 3 or more seconds.

Extending wait time also improves the quality and variety of adults' questions.

Think-Pair-Share is an effective tool for increasing wait time. It also gives children more opportunity to develop their language of learning.

- In a **pair**, children discuss possible responses.

- Volunteers are invited to **share** their ideas with the larger group.

The advantage to this approach is that your children will get more opportunity to prepare and practise the language they need before responding. By preparing independently first, then verbalising their ideas, then comparing with other children's ideas, they will have time to rehearse and formulate their views. This in turn causes your children to be more willing to contribute their ideas, make better use of language and be more willing to take intellectual risks. All of this should be encouraged in excellent early children and school settings.

NOW TRY THIS

Ask whether you can observe a learning activity being led by one of your colleagues. Don't tell them what you are looking out for yet. Record the length of time they give children to respond to questions and ideas. Audio or video record the session if possible. Afterwards, talk with your colleague about your findings and about what the two of you have learnt from the experience. Ensure all of this is done in a spirit of learning and trust. There should be no criticism, implied or otherwise.

5.1 TRUST AND RESPECT

Children trust people they think are reliable, honest and have good intentions.

Research by Bryk and Schneider (2002), amongst others, has shown that nurturing trusting relationships is one of the key features of improving children's learning. By trust, they mean the firm belief in a person's reliability, benevolence and honesty.

When trust is a part of your children's learning experiences, then they will feel able to take risks, make mistakes, express opinions and collaborate more positively with one another.

Some of the ways you can build trust and respect whilst engaging your children in some of the activities in this book include:

- Challenging, not point scoring.

- Humour and humility.

- Playful trickery.

Challenging, not point scoring

All of the activities in this book work best when trust is built upon supportive challenge.

Many of the activities in this book owe much to the Socratic tradition of education. Socrates (470–399 BCE) often posed a series of questions to help a person reflect on their underlying beliefs and the extent of their knowledge. Such questioning was not about point scoring or proving someone wrong. Indeed, it is said of Socrates that he questioned his fellow Athenians not through an arrogant sense of his being right and their being wrong but through a desire to unearth contradictions and misconceptions that were blocking the way to true wisdom.

And so it is with the activities in this book. They are not designed to make your children feel bad about what they don't know or to worry them by being in the pit: quite the reverse, actually.

Challenging Early Learning is designed to help children think more deeply and more compellingly about their learning. The activities in this book should promote a spirit of exploration to identify complexity and subtlety. They are not about point scoring but about awareness, understanding and the creation of new ideas.

Humour and humility

Humour and humility are also important ingredients in making the activities in this book work well.

Humour and humility are difficult to convey in a book, but they are absolutely key aspects of *Challenging Early Learning*.

If you were to give the impression of attempting to interrogate children during one of the learning activities in this book, then that would be very discouraging. Instead, you should take a light-hearted and self-effacing attitude. This means using phrases such as, 'Sorry, I'm not sure what you mean' or 'I don't understand; can you help me please?' It means laughing *with* rather than at your children, admitting you don't have all the answers, asking innocent questions and using a tone of voice and body language that suggest you are enjoying thinking and exploring with your children.

Playful trickery

In some ways, we are advocating a type of trickery, particularly when trying to get children into the pit (see Section 2.3). However, we only ever mean 'trickery' in the playful way that is typical of early learning. We definitely do not mean in the way that a con artist might try to trick someone. Think the coin-behind-the-ear trick rather than the watch-off-your-wrist-before-you-know-it trick!

You might also be interested to know that the root word for 'challenge' comes from the Latin *calumnia*, and it originally meant trickery!

5.2 LISTENING AND THINKING (RATHER THAN LISTENING AND *TALKING*)

Whenever we set up a *Challenging Early Learning* activity, we begin by telling the children that we would like everyone to do their best listening and thinking. We draw attention to the fact that we did not say 'listening and *talking*' but 'listening and *thinking*'. Of course, we would like the children to feel confident and interested enough to talk in front of others too. However, we know that some people do their best thinking by not talking very much. So the last thing we want to do is reduce the amount of thinking they do simply so they can concentrate on what they should say if they are put on the spot to speak!

There is a commonly held belief that educators should try to ensure all children say at least one thing in every discussion. The idea being that if they speak, then apparently we 'know' they have been concentrating. This is nonsensical, though, because children who are anxious about having to speak in front of others will concentrate *less* on what is being said! Instead, they will expend their energies on avoiding being picked to speak.

One way to explain this is through the work of Katharine Cook Briggs and her daughter, Isabel Briggs Myers. During World War II, they created the Myers-Briggs Type Indicator (MBTI) to help women identify the sort of wartime jobs in which they would be most comfortable and effective. Their work was based on the theories of Carl Jung (Briggs and Myers, 1943).

Of the four pairs of preferences proposed in the MBTI assessment tool, one set of 'opposites' focussed on the difference between 'extraversion' and 'introversion'. It identified that some people tend to 'act-reflect-act' (extraversion), whereas others 'reflect-act-reflect' (introversion). Or, put another way:

> Introverted thinking is about *thinking to talk*.
>
> Extraverted thinking is about *talking to think*.

Of course, this is a personality test and should therefore be taken with a very big pinch of salt. It is also context related: how many of us are introverted when dragged to a party of complete strangers but extroverted when playing host at our own party? Context obviously matters! So it is simply not true to say that we are either one way or the other *all the time*.

The key is that some people – children included – *typically* find it easier to think if they don't have to say anything, whereas others *typically* find talking lots helps to clarify their thinking. Contrast this with many activities in which the adult begins by saying: 'I'm going to pass this fluffy owl around the circle. When you've got it, then, and only then, is it your turn to talk!'

Imagine that you're in the mood for some introverted thinking and you've been given the fluffy owl first. What do you do? Everyone is looking at you expectantly, but you haven't had time to think about what you might say. As the pressure builds, your teacher reminds you to say 'pass' if you want to. The problem is you know if you *do* say pass, then everyone will think you're a dimwit. Meanwhile, around the other side of the circle, there's an extraverted thinker desperate to say

When starting any of the activities in this book, remind your children to listen and think.

Do *not* insist that all children talk during every activity because some children do their best thinking when there is no pressure to speak.

Briggs and Myers proposed that some people 'think to talk' whereas others 'talk to think'.

Extraverted thinkers love to think out loud so will be frustrated by having to wait their turn. Introverted thinkers prefer to think before they speak so they will be frustrated if they are pressurised to speak.

something, with words and ideas ready to pour out! Eventually, the extraverted child shouts out and the teacher barks at him for breaking the rules.

Oh, the joys of teaching! (And, yes, so very many times, we have been *that* teacher.)

Better ways to run dialogues that encourage thinking in both an extraverted *and* introverted manner include:

> **Reflection time**: Give everyone a moment to either collect her own thoughts or to share her first ideas (very quietly) with the person next to her.
>
> **Pause**: Pause the activity halfway through to give some thinking time. Do a physical activity, and then return to the activity again.
>
> **Inner circle and outer circle**: This works particularly well if you have a large group of children. Split the group in two and get half of the children to sit in a circle, with the other half sat around the outside of the circle. The outer group listen to what is being said by the inner circle. At regular intervals, you can then switch the groups around so that the inner circle children get time to listen whilst the outer circle get their chance to speak.

Of course, many of us might still worry if some children don't speak. However, we don't know that children are concentrating even if they *do* speak! Many children have learnt phrases and tactics designed to give the impression that they are focussed when actually their mind is elsewhere.

So whether you are in discussion with one child or a whole group of children, we recommend:

- Pause and reflect time.

- Feasibility language. Phrases such as 'perhaps', 'maybe', or 'I was wondering' promote a sense of open-mindedness and exploration, which is something that's vital, particularly for the children who think they need to be sure before they speak.

- Observing how the children respond to what is being said. If children laugh at the appropriate moment, nod or shake their heads in response to something someone does or in some way respond through body language to something that is being said, then the chances are that they are concentrating even if they have not spoken yet.

Here are a few ways to help both introverted and extraverted thinkers.

If children do not speak, it does not necessarily mean that they are not concentrating. The reverse is also true: those children who do speak might not be concentrating all that much (judging by some comments children make!).

NOW TRY THIS

Pay particular attention to the children who don't normally speak during activities. What outward signs are there that they are concentrating on the activity or on what other people are saying? This might include body language, eye movement, head tilts and so on. Talk with your colleagues about this and think about the question, 'Can we ever be sure which children are concentrating and which ones are not?'

5.3 DEVELOPING QUESTIONING

Questions are so contextual that it is better to avoid thinking about 'higher-order' and 'lower-order' questions. Instead, it is better to think about 'questioning' that makes use of different questions at different times for different purposes.

In Section 5.0, we mentioned research by Mary Budd Rowe (1986). What Rowe also found was that educators ask a lot of questions. In fact, she found that teachers ask on average 400 questions per day. That is a lot of questions. Imagine how positive you would feel about answering a questionnaire that consisted of 400 questions! So this section is not about increasing the number of questions. Instead, it is about increasing the quality of questioning.

Our starting point is to recommend that you resist the idea that so-called 'lower-order' questions are bad or that 'higher-order' questions are good. We believe that classifying questions into taxonomies and hierarchies steers people away from what really matters: the process and effect of questioning.

Imagine that questions were like cars. No one car is better for all purposes than another. A small city car would be best for short journeys around town but not so great for moving into a new house. An electric car would be great for green travel but not so great if there is nowhere

Figure 33: Quality questioning

Effective questioning includes more of the actions shown in the right-hand column of Figure 33.

Less of	More of
Rapid fire questions	Thoughtful questions that help children think
Questions directed to the whole group, with very few children responding	Questions directed to willing individuals
Questions that ask children to state small pieces of knowledge unrelated to other things	Questions that prompt connections between ideas
Questions that ask *what* children already know	Questions that ask *how* children know what they know
Questions with quick answers	Questions with thinking time
Questions limited to children's current understanding	Questions that extend children's understanding
Adults asking questions	Children asking questions
Answering questions straightaway	Time to reflect on and enjoy the questions themselves

to recharge its battery on route. A four-wheel drive might sound as though it would be better in snow but not if it has low-profile summer tyres on it. In other words, there are no 'higher-order' cars or 'lower-order' ones. Each has a particular purpose at which it excels, and each has ways in which it is pretty useless.

Effective questioning is an interaction. It is a process. It is about variety, purpose and flow. Your questioning should encourage children to think more. It should encourage them to wonder and engage. It should lead to their asking questions themselves. Your questioning should not be about increasing 'teacher talk' but about increasing children's learning.

Effective questioning should lead to deeper thinking and engagement.

NOW TRY THIS

Ask someone to record you working with children for a short period. We recommend 15 to 60 minutes. If you're anything like us, then you will hate seeing yourself on video but try to look past that and focus instead on your questioning techniques. Use Figure 33 to help you think about the quality of your interactions with your children and to think about what you could do next time so that those interactions were even better.

5.4 OPEN-ENDED QUESTIONS

In the previous section, we said that the purpose and quality of questioning are far more important than the type of questions asked. Having said that, some questions typically (though not always) help to extend children's thinking. These are sometimes called Socratic questions or open-ended questions. We will share both types here.

Open questions are designed to encourage children to give fuller, more meaningful answers that make connections to other ideas or feelings. They are the opposite of closed questions that encourage a short or single-word answer. Of course, the success of the open questions will depend on your questioning techniques. Assuming, though, that you are giving time for thinking, encouraging exploration and intellectual risk taking, then the following questions could help extend children's learning:

If the purpose of your questioning is to deepen learning, then open-ended questions can often help.

What are you doing?

Can you describe what is happening?

Can you think of a new way to do it?

Who can think of another idea?

Why did that happen?

What do you think might happen next?

How did you get that to work?

How are they alike?

How are they different?

Which one is the best one and why?

How does it make you feel?

What was it like learning together?

What could you do differently next time?

What did you learn?

What was the hardest thing about it?

What was the easiest thing about it?

What was the most interesting thing?

5.5 SOCRATIC QUESTIONS

Socratic questions are some of the most tried and tested examples of open questions.

Socratic questions come from the techniques reputedly used by the ancient Greek philosopher Socrates (470–399 BC), who asked searching questions about such essential concepts as courage, beauty and a good life.

We have organised them into categories around a mnemonic 'CRAVE Questions' that James first used in his original book, *Challenging Learning* (2010). This way of organising them should help you refer to them more productively whilst working with your children.

Socratic questions can be categorised into six types: those that seek clarification, reasons, assumptions, viewpoints, effects and metacognition.

These questions are very useful for creating cognitive conflict as well as for helping your children to climb out of the pit (see Section 2.3). We would strongly recommend that you display these examples on your nursery walls so that you can easily refer to them whilst interacting with your children. That will make it much more likely that the questioning techniques will become part of everyday practice.

The mnemonic stands for:

Clarification.

Reasons.

Assumptions.

Viewpoints.

Effects.

Questions (questions about questions, metacognition).

C – clarification: Questions that encourage clarity and depth

- What does that mean?
- How does this relate to what we have been talking about?
- What do we already know about this?
- Are you saying . . . or . . . ?
- Can you say that in a different way please?

R – reasons: Questions that check whether reasons support conclusions

- Why are you saying that?
- Why is . . . happening?
- What other reasons might there be?
- Can you give us an example?
- Are your reasons good ones?

A – assumptions: Questions that check presuppositions and unquestioned beliefs

- What are you assuming?
- Did you think that that would happen?
- What would happen if . . . ?
- Do you agree or disagree with . . . ?
- So, are you thinking that. . . ?

V – viewpoints: Questions that seek to find alternative interpretations of a situation

- Is there another way to look at this?
- What would your friend say about this?
- Who do you think might change this?
- What are the best bits and worst bits about it?
- How could you look at this in another way?

E – effects: Questions designed to reveal consequences and implications

- What do you think will happen next?
- If we do this then what would happen?
- How does this affect that?
- What could we change so that it gives us a different outcome?
- If you do that, what do you expect to see?

Q – questions: Questions about questions (metacognition)

- How effective was your question?
- Which of your questions turned out to be the most useful?
- Why do you think he asked that question?
- Can you improve any of the questions you've heard today?
- What would you do to improve your questions in future?

5.6 WHO, WHAT, WHERE, WHEN, WHY, HOW

A nice way to build up questioning skills with your children is to use the format shown in Figure 34 after reading a story together.

Questioning can be even more effective when children learn how to ask their own questions that extend their learning.

Figure 34: Top six story questions

Who	Who was the main character?
What	What did they do?
Where	Where did they go?
When	When did the story get most exciting?
Why	Why was the story a good one?
How	How would you change the story to make it even better?

NOW TRY THIS

Think of three or four more questions that could go with each of the six CRAVE Question categories. Try each alternative you come up with over the coming weeks, and then talk with a colleague about which ones work best for your children and why.

5.7 QUESTION STEMS

These question stems are building blocks that can help children develop their own questioning techniques.

Other useful question stems include those shown in Figure 35. Again, we suggest that you display these on your nursery or school walls for your easy reference. This will help you to generate questions that challenge and engage your children.

A good way to use these questions stems is to pick a different one each week. Then you can help your children get into the habit of using that particular question stem before learning a new one. As time goes on, they will build up their questioning skills so that it becomes part of who they are and what they do.

For another explanation of how you can help your children develop these sorts of attitudes, we encourage you to read Section 6.2, example 5.7.

5.8 THINKING PROGRESS

The purpose of questioning in learning is to extend and build children's understanding. Figure 36 shows what impact this might have on children's language skills.

There are many ways to think about progress in children's thinking. Figure 36 gives some ideas.

Figure 35: Creating questions

Question stem	Example
What is . . . ?	What is a **pet**?
How do we know what . . . is?	How do we know what **happiness** is?
Who says what . . . is?	Who says what **toys** are?
What makes . . . ?	What makes something **nice**?
Would you be . . . ?	Would you be **rude** if you didn't laugh at a joke?
Always or never	Should we always **share** things? (Germs? Ideas?)
Always or never	Should we never tell **lies**?
What if . . . ?	What if **animals** could talk to humans?
Is it possible . . . ?	Is it possible to be **happy** all the time?
How is . . . ?	How are **dreams** different from thinking?
When . . . ?	When is **choice** a bad thing?
Who . . . ?	Who decides what **fairness** is?
Can we . . . ?	Can we think without **words**?
What is the difference between . . . ?	What is the difference between a **story** and a **fairy tale**?

Figure 36: Progression in thinking

Emerging	Developing	Extending
talk	discuss	debate
work together	cooperate	collaborate
give reasons	explain	justify
think	concentrate	focus
choose	decide	conclude
take turns	include	involve
make links	make connections	understand connections
ask questions	make sense of	explain
answer questions	respond	connect
remember	recall	link

5.9 CHAPTER SUMMARY

This chapter has covered the following main points:

1 All children should be encouraged to wonder, elaborate and pause for thought.

2 Mary Budd Rowe (1986) found that the average amount of time an adult waits after asking children a question before asking another question or giving a prompt is one second or less.

3 When adults wait for a minimum of 3 seconds *before* taking an answer from their children and then wait another 3 seconds *after* taking an answer, the effects are powerfully positive.

4 Some children prefer to think carefully before talking. This can mean that putting children on the spot and requiring them to talk can be counterproductive to the learning process. It is better to give lots of thinking time and then to invite volunteers to speak.

5 By the same token, some children do their best thinking out loud. So it is counterproductive to stop those children from talking! Instead, we should give lots of opportunity for them to express their thoughts. This can include whispering their ideas or talking to a partner before sharing with the wider group and so on.

6 It is sensible to resist the idea that so-called lower-order questions are bad or that higher-order questions are good. The key to learning is less about the questions and more about the process of *questioning*.

7 Effective questioning is an interaction. It is a process. It is about variety, purpose and flow.

6. MAKING PROGRESS

PLAY IS THE ANSWER TO HOW ANYTHING NEW COMES ABOUT.

(Jean Piaget, 1955)

6.0 FOCUS ON PROGRESS

All the ideas in this book are focussed on helping young children to grow and flourish. Another way to say this is that they are all geared towards children making progress.

By 'making progress', we mean gains in proficiency. Examples in this book include helping young children improve their attitudes, skills and knowledge for learning; supporting adults to improve their questioning skills; and using different strategies for enhancing the learning environment so that everyone might benefit.

However, to say that education should be focussed on progress seems a pretty obvious thing to say. Yet reality doesn't seem quite so straightforward. Take, for example, a situation in which a child shows that he can tie his shoelaces or ride a bike. Should we praise him for these abilities? Should we say, 'That is great; well done you!' Most of us would probably say yes – that is, if we didn't suspect that the question being asked was a trick one!

It is indeed a trick question because what if the skill we are praising them for is an easy one *for them*? What if it was their 'easy path' as shown in Figure 7 (page 17)? How would you feel if you were praised for tying your shoelaces or riding a bike? You'd think whoever was praising you was being sarcastic or patronising. Or both.

> Most of us wouldn't praise children for doing something that they find straightforward and easy.

Yet, how often does this happen in the lives of children and not just in our nursery and school settings? Think of the schoolchildren who are praised for getting full marks in a test even if that test is easy for them. Or the most articulate ones who are praised for volunteering answers more than others. Or the most skilful players who are praised for consistently scoring more points than others. These situations are so common that perhaps it just seems the right thing to do. And yet, as we explored in Chapter 2, these are some of the very reasons why so many children choose to stay in their comfort zone. They think that the better they perform, the greater the chance that adults will praise them. So to maximise their chances of performing well, they play it safe and only choose to do things that they can already do. The 'clever' kids seek out the tests they know they can ace; the 'articulate' kids volunteer only when they can find the right words to use; and the 'dexterous' kids always want to be on the same team as the other skilful kids! There is another way, though.

> And yet in schools, a lot of teachers will reward students who get everything right even if the task was completed effortlessly.

The alternative is to focus on the progress your children are making. So rather than looking at the end result, instead we look at the journey they have made to get there. We identify where they have started and where they are got to. We talk about their personal best rather than who is better than whom. We encourage them to improve, but the main competition is against themselves rather than against one another.

> We should avoid praising children for easy success. Instead, we should show delight when they make progress in more demanding activities.

Here are some examples for you to choose between.

Single piece of art

Rather than displaying just the finished artwork, show the children's progress from starting point to finished piece with any improvements in between. (See Figure 37.)

Figure 37: Photographs showing progress in one piece of artwork

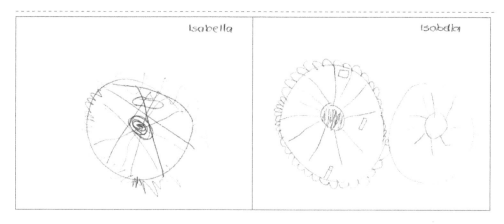

Figure 38: Showing longer-term progress in art

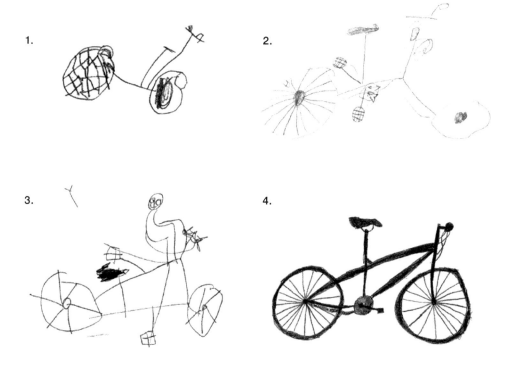

Developing artwork

Collect a series of drawings from the children over a period of weeks, then display the improvements side by side.

Figure 38 shows the progress in drawing by a child, starting from when he was five (drawing 1) to when he was seven (drawing 4).

Models and modelling

The same idea applies to models that the children make. You can photograph the process of building a model and then create a display showing steps along the way to the completed model. Or you could take photographs of objects children build over a series of weeks or months. Then create a display showing the increasing complexity of their models. (See Figure 39.)

Figure 39: Photographs showing progress in model building

Taking photographs as children build models and then using them to tell the story of progress can be an effective way to draw attention to the process of learning.

Figure 40: What is science? Week 1

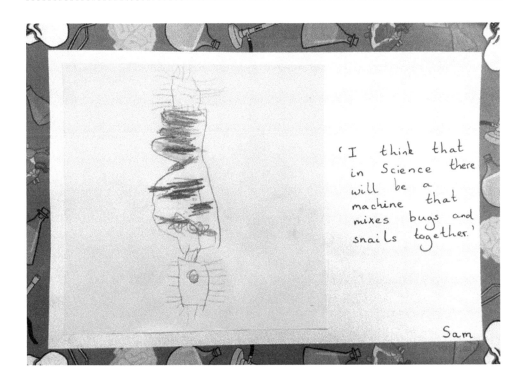

'I think that in Science there will be a machine that mixes bugs and snails together.'

Sam

Progress in understanding

We love this example from Dulwich Prep School in London. Figure 40 is a drawing by Sam together with the words he spoke when asked the question, 'What do you think "science" is all about?' Figure 41 shows his responses to the same question six weeks later after he'd taken part in some science lessons in his Early Years setting. When both of these responses are displayed side by side, it draws attention very nicely to the emphasis the school has on progress.

Nan's butterfly

The video of 'Austin's Butterfly' is a well-known clip on YouTube in which Ron Berger invites feedback from children at Presumpscot Elementary School in Portland, Maine. Their advice helps Austin to improve his drawing of a butterfly. Inspired by this, Nana Roger ran a similar project with children at Børnehuset Sneglehuset, Frederiksberg in Denmark.

Figure 41: What is science? Week 6

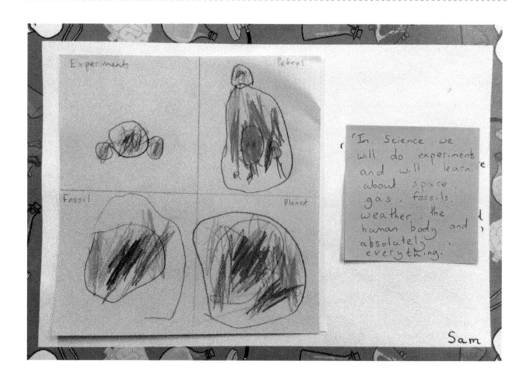

As Nana reports: 'I invited 5-year-old Silja to pick an image of a butterfly that she liked online (Figure 42) and then to create a copy of it'. Her first attempt can be seen in Figure 43. 'Then one by one, her friends gave her feedback, and Silja drew another version of the butterfly'. Figures 44–46 show the progression. As with all the other examples in this chapter, displaying the different attempts side by side helps to emphasise and celebrate the importance of progress in children's learning.

Figure 42: Nana's butterfly

Figure 43: Silja's butterfly, Version 1

Figure 44: Silja's butterfly, Version 2

Figure 45: Silja's butterfly, Version 3

Figure 46: Silja's butterfly, Version 4

Story writing

The next example comes from Brudenell Primary School in Leeds. They routinely give children the same activity months apart so that they can more clearly see the progress being made. This is then celebrated with the child and his or her parents and influences the next steps in the teaching. Figure 47 shows the progress Jessica, aged five, made between July one year and May the following year.

Daily diaries

Create daily diaries for all your children. These can share details of the activities and learning experiences that the children have been involved in. At end of the week, draw attention to the

Figure 47: Progress in story writing by Jessica, aged five

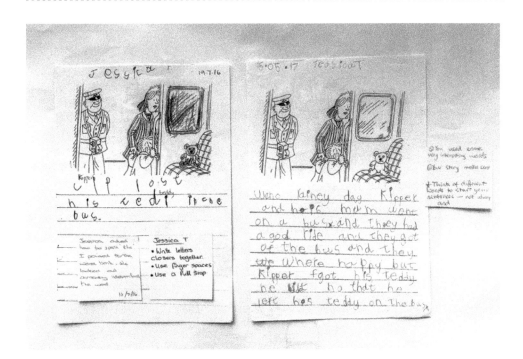

progress the children have made in terms of one or two key points. For example, 'Sam has learned to zip up his own coat and is becoming more and more confident in climbing on the wooden frames outside'.

Thinking journals

Create thinking journals for your children within which they draw their thoughts following different learning activities. They can add further ideas over time or extend their original ideas that they recorded earlier in their journal. These journals will show the children, their parents and you how their ideas are gaining in complexity over time.

Learning folders

Give each child a large folder with a photograph of themselves on the front. Then use this to collect examples of their learning throughout the year. This can be added to by you, by the children and by the children's parents. It can also be used when they move to the next room or group as they get older.

Learning conferences

Host learning conferences in which children show their parents the progress they have been making recently. This gives your children the opportunity to show examples of what they have been learning and improving. If used in conjunction with some of the other ideas here, then each child should have many examples to showcase.

Growing confidence

Record some of the activities that children are engaged in. Look for signs of increasing confidence. This might include asking more questions, giving longer answers, being more willing to say no thank you and so on. This could run in conjunction with the Learning Detectives idea shown in Section 1.6.

Diaries, thinking journals and learning folders are popular ways for tracking and sharing children's progress in learning.

Inviting children to take part in parents' meetings gives them the opportunity to talk about their own progress in learning.

Reading

Create a record of the words that a child has learnt to read over a period of time. This can be in the form of a Progress Tree where each new sound/word is written on a leaf. (See Figure 48.) As the tree fills up with leaves, the child can see the progress she is making. As new phases of reading are started, a new tree can be drawn, or different coloured leaves can be added to the original tree.

Figure 48: A Progress Tree for reading

Figure 49: A Progress Arrow for numeracy

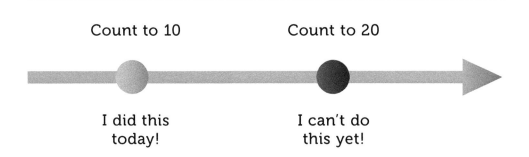

Count to 10   Count to 20

I did this today!   I can't do this yet!

Personal care

Create some cardboard cut-outs of people. As your children master each stage of dressing, manipulating buttons, zips, laces and so on, they can add images relating to that skill to their own cardboard character. For examples, once they have learnt to fasten their outdoor coat independently, they can draw a coat to put on their character.

Numeracy

Create Progress Arrows that show where children are in terms of numeracy skills. For example, one child's Progress Arrow might look like the one shown in Figure 49.

Sports Day

During PE lessons, record your children's performances over a few months. For example, how fast they can run 30 metres, how far they can jump, how fast they can run the egg-and-spoon race and so on. Then on Sports Day, record their performances and hand out prizes to every child beating their PB (personal best).

Sports Day does not have to be viewed as a one-off event. Instead, if you record children's performances over a number of weeks, Sports Day can become a celebration of children beating their own personal bests.

Version 2.0

Every month, get out something that your children created the month before. Then invite them to use their newly improved skills and understanding to edit their original creations in order to make them even better than they were before. Examples include paintings, drawings, writing, letter formations and so on.

6.1 PROGRESS IN TERMS OF THE SOLO TAXONOMY

The SOLO Taxonomy is a very useful way to think about progress in learning. SOLO stands for the Structure of the Observed Learning Outcome. John Biggs and Kevin Collis first described it in *Evaluating the Quality of Learning: The SOLO Taxonomy* (1982).

The SOLO Taxonomy can help to describe a person's progress from surface-level knowledge to deep understanding. There are five stages in the model (Figure 50).

To help you understand the SOLO Taxonomy better, we have applied it to three more contexts familiar to young children in Figures 51, 52 and 53.

The SOLO Taxonomy is a simple and effective way to describe progress in learning.

Figure 50 gives an overview of the SOLO Taxonomy. Figures 51, 52 and 53 give examples of how the SOLO Taxonomy applies to popular topics for three- to seven-year-olds.

Figure 50: Progress in terms of the SOLO Taxonomy

SOLO Stage

Prestructural

Unistructural

Multistructural

Relational

Extended Abstract

NO IDEA
SOLO Term: Prestructural

Your children know nothing about the topic. For example, they have no idea what mini-beasts (invertebrates) are.

ONE IDEA
SOLO Term: Unistructural

Your children know one or two things about the topic. For example, they know that wasps and spiders are mini-beasts.

MANY IDEAS
SOLO Term: Multistructural

Your children know lots of things about the topic. For example, they know that mini-beasts are small animals such as spiders, slugs, snails, beetles, insects, centipedes and so on; they know that none of them have backbones and that there are more mini-beasts than any other creature on earth.

CONNECTING IDEAS
SOLO Term: Relational

Your children understand how the ideas they have learned relate and connect to each other. For example, they can explain similarities and differences between different mini-beasts including number of legs, whether they have a shell or not antennae or not and where they live.

REVIEWING & EXTENDING IDEAS
SOLO Term: Extended Abstract

Your children can extend and apply their understanding to new contexts. For example, they can draw distinctions between mini-beasts and other creatures such as birds, fish and mammals; they can also design superheroes that have the talents and qualities of various mini-beasts.

Figure 51: The SOLO Taxonomy and colours

SOLO Stage

Prestructural

NO IDEA
SOLO Term: Prestructural

Your children cannot name any colours.

Unistructural

ONE IDEA
SOLO Term: Unistructural

Your children know the names of, and can recognise, basic colours such as red, yellow and blue.

Multistructural

MANY IDEAS
SOLO Term: Multistructural

Your children know the names of, and can recognise, most common colours including red, yellow, blue, green, orange, purple, black, white, pink and brown. They can also give examples of objects normally associated with that colour (for example, yellow bananas and green grass).

Relational

CONNECTING IDEAS
SOLO Term: Relational

Your children understand how to make new colours by mixing other colours. They can predict that mixing red and yellow makes orange: red and blue makes purple; red and white makes pink; and so on.

Extended Abstract

REVIEWING & EXTENDING IDEAS
SOLO Term: Extended Abstract

Your children can explain the significance of colours. For example, red is used for danger, yellow for happiness, green for go and so on. They understand that there are many shades of colour and can group these accordingly (for example, light blue, bright blue, pale blue and so on).

Figure 52: The SOLO Taxonomy about dressing for the outdoors

SOLO Stage	
Prestructural	**NO IDEA** SOLO Term: Prestructural Your children have never dressed themselves; an adult always does it for them.
Unistructural	**ONE IDEA** SOLO Term: Unistructural Your children can find their outdoor clothes to put on but don't know what to do next.
Multistructural 	**MANY IDEAS** SOLO Term: Multistructural Your children can put their outdoor trousers, coat and boots on. They can zip their coat up and can put their hat and gloves on independently.
Relational 	**CONNECTING IDEAS** SOLO Term: Relational Your children can explain how they were able to get dressed and ready for the outdoors.
Extended Abstract 	**REVIEWING & EXTENDING IDEAS** SOLO Term: Extended Abstract Your children can teach others how to get ready for outdoor play.

Figure 53: The SOLO Taxonomy about seasons

SOLO Stage	
Prestructural	**NO IDEA** SOLO Term: Prestructural Your children cannot name any seasons.
Unistructural	**ONE IDEA** SOLO Term: Unistructural Your children know the names of summer and winter (and maybe spring and autumn) but do not know the significance of these.
Multistructural 	**MANY IDEAS** SOLO Term: Multistructural Your children know the names of the seasons and can describe the weather normally associated with each one.
Relational 	**CONNECTING IDEAS** SOLO Term: Relational Your children understand the sequence of seasons (for example, that spring follows winter). They can also link some of the festivals in their culture to seasons (for example, Christmas in winter, Easter in spring, Diwali in autumn, and so on*).
Extended Abstract 	**REVIEWING & EXTENDING IDEAS** SOLO Term: Extended Abstract Your children make links to seasonal foods, farming, harvesting and so on. They can also link the months of the year to their relative season.

* Reversed for those in the southern hemisphere of course!

NOW TRY THIS

Pick one of the following themes. With a colleague, complete the SOLO Taxonomy template shown in Figure 54.

1 Alphabet

2 Animals

- Farm animals
- Wild animals
- Woodland animals
- Zoo animals

3 Castles

4 Celebrations

5 Dinosaurs

6 Family

7 Farming

8 Gardening

9 Growing

10 Houses and homes

11 Hygiene

12 Kings and queens

13 Night and day

14 Oceans and seas

15 Opposites

16 Rainforest

17 Recipes

18 Recycling

19 Seaside

20 Senses

21 Shape

22 Space and planets

23 Towns and cities

24 Transport

Figure 54: SOLO Taxonomy template

We have left Figure 54 blank so that you can photocopy it before using it to plan children's progress in any given topic.

SOLO Stage	
Prestructural	NO IDEA SOLO Term: Prestructural
Unistructural 	ONE IDEA SOLO Term: Unistructural
Multistructural 	MANY IDEAS SOLO Term: Multistructural
Relational 	CONNECTING IDEAS SOLO Term: Relational
Extended Abstract 	REVIEWING & EXTENDING IDEAS SOLO Term: Extended Abstract

6.2 THE SOLO TAXONOMY AND LEARNING

Throughout this book, we have offered recommendations for ways in which you can help your children learn. As we've mentioned before, none of these suggestions have been made in the spirit of pushing children or hothousing them. Instead, we have offered the ideas with the intention of adding to what you already do to help children flourish. The SOLO Taxonomy can help to explain this further.

Each of the ideas in this book is shared with the intention of helping children progress from . . .

not being aware of, to . . .

becoming familiar with, to . . .

really understanding or being proficient at, to . . .

being creative in how . . . .

Here are examples of how the SOLO Taxonomy can be used to show progress in some of the ideas shared earlier in the book.

This can apply just as well in terms of attitudes, skills or knowledge. Going back over the book, here are some examples of what we mean:

Example number	Section	Examples
1	1.4	If we select one of the ASK attitudes such as 'determination', then the SOLO Taxonomy can help us think about supporting children in moving from having no determination for learning; to being determined when the mood suits them; to being determined in all aspects of learning; to understanding how determination can affect the outcome of what they are doing; to choosing how and when and why to be determined and when to compromise.
2	1.6	The key to the Learning Detectives is to help children think about their learning. Their growth in using this strategy can be thought about in terms of SOLO Taxonomy: to start with, they won't know what to do; then they will find out that the idea is to look for what other children are doing; as they progress to the 'multistructural' stage, they will know how to be a Learning Detective and what sorts of learning behaviours they should look for; after that, they will understand the link between what they are looking for and how this affects learning generally; finally, they think about how they are learning and what they could do to improve that learning even when they are not acting as Learning Detectives.
3	2.3	The Learning Challenge links stage for stage with the SOLO Taxonomy. This will be explored in Section 6.3. However, looking at the example concept of 'real' in that section, the SOLO Taxonomy can be used to plan ways to help children deepen their understanding of concepts such as this one. For example, at the prestructurual stage, children will not know what 'real' means; then they will move to knowing that it has something to do with existing (even though they probably won't have the language to explain this); then to knowing that real means it is true, that it is not pretend, and that it can probably be seen somehow. From there, they will progress onto understanding the similarities and differences between real and pretend and between real and true. Finally, they will be able to give examples of things that are in some ways real and in other ways not real (for example, role play), and they will begin to use 'real' in everyday situations with purpose and clarity.
4	3.5	Section 3.5 gives recommendations for ways to increase the use of exploratory talk. In SOLO Taxonomy terms, this means helping children move from not knowing how to engage in exploratory talk; to knowing that they should listen carefully to others and not interrupt; to being able to engage in exploratory talk by giving reasons, longer explanations, asking questions and being collaborative. After that, the progress would involve being more 'natural' in their use of exploratory

talk so that they no longer need reminding to use it; to eventually, to understanding how exploratory talk gives much more satisfactory results than any other type of dialogue. Of course, young children won't use terms such as 'exploratory' talk, but they should nonetheless be able to learn the techniques of this type of talk so long as they get the right support and encouragement (and role modelling) from the adults around them.

5   5.7   Chapter 5 shares ways to help adults and children develop their questioning skills. Section 5.7 gives some example question stems that can be used as building blocks for questions. In SOLO Taxonomy terms, this means helping children move from not knowing what a question is; to recognising when simple questions are being asked; to being able to recognise and respond appropriately to more complex questions; to being able to use rehearsed questions appropriately; and finally to being able to create and use their own purposeful questions in a range of contexts.

NOW TRY THIS

Choose one of the concepts in the prepared questions list appearing in Section 2.5.3. Describe the progress children could make in their understanding of that concept by using the SOLO Taxonomy levels as just shown.

6.3 THE SOLO TAXONOMY AND THE LEARNING CHALLENGE

The SOLO Taxonomy links stage for stage with the Learning Challenge that we shared in Sections 2.3 to 2.7. Figure 55 gives an overview of this.

The SOLO Taxonomy and the Learning Challenge fit very well together, as Figure 55 and the following descriptions show.

Figure 55: The Learning Challenge and the SOLO Taxonomy

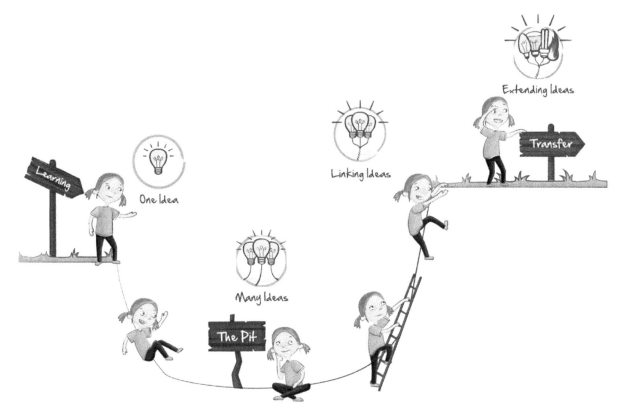

The way in which each stage of Learning Challenge works with the SOLO Taxonomy can be summarised as follows.

No idea

SOLO term: prestructural

Learning Challenge: Stage 0

This is when your children have no idea about the topic. At this stage, the Learning Challenge will *not* work. Before you can get your children into the pit, they will need at least *some* idea about the concept in question. For example, you will not be able to get four-year-olds into the pit about a concept as complex as gravity because it is very unlikely that they will have the faintest idea what gravity is!

One idea

SOLO term: unistructural

Learning Challenge: Stage 1

This is when your children have one idea or at least a basic set of notions about the topic. At this stage, the Learning Challenge is ready to begin. Generally, you can start by asking what the concept means. So, for example, 'What is a friend?' or 'What is a pet?' And as long as *some* of your children (and not just the most advanced) are able to give a reasonably accurate answer involving one or two facts about the concept, then the Learning Challenge can begin.

Many ideas

SOLO term: multistructural

Learning Challenge: Stage 2

This is when your children have many ideas about the topic in question. At this stage, your children will be heading down into the pit, if they are not there already. Generally, you will have encouraged them into the pit by helping them to find ideas that conflict with their original idea. For example, 'You say that friends are people you know, but you know lots of people who aren't your friends, don't you?'

Connecting ideas

SOLO term: relational

Learning Challenge: Stage 3

This is when your children begin to connect their ideas and understand the relationships between them. In Learning Challenge terms, this is when your children construct understanding to the point of reaching a 'eureka' moment. With this new-found sense of clarity and meaning, your children will feel a sense of accomplishment, and their answers or competencies will be noticeably more developed.

Reviewing and linking ideas

SOLO   term: extended abstract

Learning   Challenge: Stage 4

This is when your children extend and apply their understanding to new contexts. In Learning Challenge terms, this is the point at which they look to blend their new discoveries with past knowledge so that they might better understand the bigger picture. They also innovate and create new applications for their understanding.

6.4 PROGRESS AND A GROWTH MINDSET

Carol Dweck is professor of psychology at Stanford University and author of the best-selling book *Mindset* (2006). From over 30 years of research, she has found that some people believe their success is based on innate ability; she says these people have a fixed theory of intelligence. Other people believe their success is based on hard work and learning. Dweck says these people have a 'growth' or 'incremental' theory of intelligence.

The idea of fixed and growth mindset was developed by Carol Dweck from a lifetime of careful and precise research.

When people believe that their intelligence is more or less constant throughout their lives, then this can cause them to:

- Worry about how much intelligence or ability they have.

- Focus on showing that they are more intelligent or able than others.

- Choose to do things that are easy for them so that they look clever.

- Respond negatively to setbacks and challenges.

- Perceive feedback as criticism.

In a fixed mindset, people believe that talents and abilities are relatively constant.

When people think and act in this way, Professor Dweck would say they are in a 'fixed' mindset.

However, when people believe that intelligence and abilities are not something they 'possess' but something they enhance through learning, then they tend to:

- Focus on learning and improving.

- Choose things that will stretch and challenge them.

- Seek ways to put their talents to good use.

- Look for ways to learn from setbacks and challenges.

- Perceive feedback as information that they can learn from.

In a growth mindset, people believe that talents and abilities are developed and malleable.

People enjoy learning more when they are in a growth mindset.

When people think and act in this way, Professor Dweck would say they are in a 'growth' mindset.

Mindset is as applicable to children as it is to adults, although perhaps the younger children are, the less likely they are to be in a fixed mindset. We say this because very rarely do babies and toddlers display anything other than a willingness to try new things, to explore, to experiment. However, as children grow older, they become far more aware of what 'normal' expectations are for their abilities. This leads very many to compare themselves with others and to realise that some people are better at some things and others are worse at those exact same things. Trying to make sense of this, they look for explanations, and all too often, they see only 'natural' differences rather than the difference in progress made so far.

Although most young children tend to be in a growth mindset, too many then lean towards a fixed mindset later in life.

As someone who works with children, you have a significant impact on the mindset that your young charges are likely to be in. You won't be the only influence, of course; the children's parents are likely to have a much greater impact. However, as we wrote about in Section 1.0 when talking about playgroup versus Little Acorns, you *significantly* influence how your children think and behave. If you emphasise learning, progress, enjoyment of challenge and the welcoming of advice, then your children are much more likely to be in a growth mindset. Whereas if you emphasise natural abilities, comparisons between children, avoidance of challenge and negative feelings towards mistakes, then your children are much more likely to be in a fixed mindset.

We can do many things as adults to help young children continue to see the world through a growth mindset.

It is also worth bearing in mind that mindset is context specific. Indeed, it is extremely common for people to lean towards a fixed mindset in some contexts and towards a growth mindset in others. Our eldest daughter is a prime example: she tends to be in a growth mindset when swimming but in a fixed mindset when doing maths. Whenever she comes up against a problem that she can't immediately solve, in swimming she tells herself, 'There is a way to do this; I just need to find the solution'. In maths, however, she tells herself, 'Here is yet more proof that I can't do maths'. Guess which context she is making more progress in?

Mindset is not a personality trait; it is a way of thinking in a particular circumstance.

So, although we can't hope to affect every part of a child's thinking, we can very definitely have a significant impact on her thinking whilst in the educational setting. Then we will have to hope and trust that the schools will pick up where we leave off.

James regularly goes on presentation tours with Professor Dweck. He is also co-authoring a book on *Mindset* that is due out in 2018. So, for an in-depth guide to Dweck's work, we recommend you look out for that. In the meantime, the following three sections offer you things to think about that will help you help your young children.

6.5 MINDSET AND PRAISE

These common words of praise are more likely to lead children into a fixed mindset:

Praise has a particularly strong influence on which mindset children will lean towards later in life.

- Clever girl
- Good boy
- You're the best
- You're a natural
- She's gifted
- The best reader

That is not to say that praise is a bad thing. It is to say that we should direct our praise to the *actions* of the child rather than to the child himself. Before we explain this further, it would be worth looking at one of Dweck's many research studies. This one involved 10-, 11- and 12-year-olds, but Dweck and her associates have done many studies with younger children too. That said, this study is particularly clear, so it is a good place to begin.

The specifics of this are taken from an article Carol Dweck wrote with Claudia Mueller for the *Journal of Personality and Social Psychology* in 1998. In it, they describe a series of six tests they did to discover the effect of praise on children's performance.

This study by Professor Dweck involved 10- to 12-year-olds. There are many other studies involving Early Years children.

The first test involved 128 fifth-graders (70 girls and 58 boys, aged 10–12 years). Each child was seen individually by one of four experimenters. After being escorted from their usual classroom to an empty one, they were introduced to the task. They were given a brief guide to problem solving and then asked to solve 10 moderately difficult questions in four minutes.

As soon as the time was up, the adult marked the test and told the child she had done well:

> Wow, you did very well on these problems. You got [number of problems] right. That's a really high score.

Regardless of their actual score, all children were told that they had solved at least 80% of the questions they had answered.

Each child then received one of three types of praise, as follows:

Approximately one-third of the children were given **Intelligence Praise** – they were told they had done well 'because they were clever'.

Approximately one-third of the children were given **Process Praise** – they were told they had done well 'because they had tried hard'.

Approximately one-third of the children were the **control group** – they were told they had done well but were given no further explanation as to why.

Each child was then given another test, this time far more difficult. Every child struggled.

They were then told they had performed 'a lot worse' on the second test than on the first test.

After receiving this negative feedback, each child was asked to work on the third and final set of problems. These were of the same standard as the first set (moderate difficulty), so it could

Figure 56: Results of three tests given to 10- to 12-year-olds

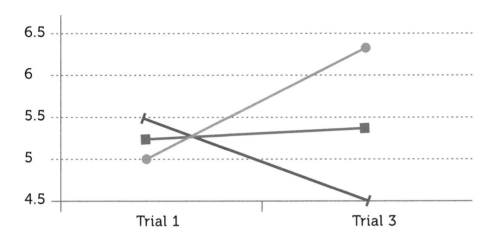

The numbers down the left show the average score out of 10 achieved by the groups of children.

Red Line – children who received **intelligence** praise

Green Line – children who received **process** praise

Orange Line – children in the **control** group

be reasonably expected that each child would have got the same score as they had on the first test. Except they didn't.

The graph in Figure 56 shows how the children's scores changed from the first set of problems to the third set of problems, after receiving the different types of praise.

As you will see from Figure 56:

- The children who were praised for being clever did worse on the third test than they had on the first test.

- The children who were praised for having tried hard did better on the third test than they had on the first test.

- The children in the control group did slightly better over time, probably because they were getting used to taking the tests.

In this study, the children who were praised for their intelligence scored worse in the third test whereas those who were praised for effort fared better.

NOW TRY THIS

Talk with one of your colleagues about the results shown in Figure 56. Think of reasons why children who were praised for being clever after doing well on the first test then performed worse in the third test, whereas those children who were praised for trying hard after doing well on the first test then performed even better in the third test.

Some of the ways to explain these findings include:

When the children praised for being clever after doing well in the first test then did badly in the second test, they began thinking that they weren't so clever after all. This led to a crisis of confidence as they began the third test.

When the children praised for having tried hard after doing well in the first test then did badly in the second test, they began thinking that they needed to try harder next time. This led to increased determination as they began the third test.

If a child succeeds because he is clever, then what does that make him when he fails? He must be stupid.

When a child succeeds because she tried hard, then what does that tell her when she fails? She needs to try harder.

Many people believe that clever people don't struggle. So, when the children who were praised for being clever started to do badly on the second test, they began thinking that they were obviously not very clever.

Many people believe that success comes from trying hard. So, when the children who were praised for trying hard started to do badly on the second test, they began thinking that they needed to try even harder.

Those children who believed they were clever decided the tests were stupid and that they did not need to prove themselves. They were also more likely to suspect that the tests were 'tricks' designed to catch them out.

> When we explain success in terms of intelligence, children are likely to think that failure is due to lack of intelligence.
>
> If we explain success in terms of correct actions, then children are likely to think that failure is due to incorrect actions.

Perhaps the most significant factor to add to this list is the sense of control or lack of control over the outcomes. When those children who were praised for being smart after the first test were told they had done badly on the second test, they must have thought to themselves, 'What can I do about it? I can't make myself smarter'. Whereas those who were praised for having tried hard after the first test were told they had done badly on the second test, they must have thought to themselves, 'I can change that; I can put more effort in right now'. In other words, the second group had the notion that they could influence outcomes through their own endeavours whereas the first group felt relatively powerless to effect a new outcome. These varying degrees of potency are often referred to as 'self-efficacy' and will be explored in more depth in Section 6.6.

> The important distinction is that children know they can change their actions more readily than they can change their level of intelligence. In other words, praising intelligence removes control, whereas praising actions puts children in the driver's seat.

Note about the test conditions:

During the debriefing given at the end of the experimental session, all children were informed that the second problem set contained problems of increased difficulty, which were considered to be appropriate for older, seventh-grade students. In fact, they were told that answering even one of these difficult problems was quite an achievement for students in their grade level. Thus, they were assured of the overall high quality of their task performance. Extensive precautions were taken to ensure that all children left the experimental setting proud of their performance.

(Mueller & Dweck, 1998, p. 36)

6.6 WAYS TO PRAISE

> Dweck's message is clear: do *not* praise children; praise their actions instead.

The key to praise that is more likely to put children into a growth mindset is to focus on actions rather than on entities. In other words, praise what children do rather than who they are. This means:

No	Yes
Clever girl	What a clever way to do it.
Good boy	That was a good thing to do.
You're the best	You're getting better all the time.
You're a natural	You've developed a wonderful talent.
Brilliant reader	Brilliant reading.

Notice in the last example that we're suggesting 'brilliant reading' rather than 'brilliant reader'. In other words, we encourage you to use the verb rather than the noun. Examples include:

Brilliant 'running' rather than brilliant 'runner'.

She loves 'being creative' rather than she 'is so creative'.

Wonderful 'writing' rather than wonderful 'writer'.

'Showing' confidence rather than 'being' confident.

To some people, this seems unnecessarily picky. We do not mean to be. It is just that most of us who work with children already know the theory about what to avoid when criticising children. We know that we should not say, 'You're a naughty child'. Instead we ought to say, 'That was a naughty thing to do'. The same can be said of praise: instead of praising the child, we should praise their actions. Though it might not feel particularly significant in the short term, in the long term, praising actions is much more likely to put children into a growth mindset and give them a sense of control over their own outcomes.

(James): Incidentally, please don't respond the way I responded when first reading Dweck's work: I stopped praising the children I was working with for fear of getting it wrong! What a fixed mindset attitude that was! I thought to myself that, seeing as I had made a mistake with every single child I'd ever worked with by calling them all clever, talented, little geniuses, I should give up the day job and go back to working on a pig farm! Obviously, that is not what Dweck is suggesting. Instead, her work recommends not that we stop praising but that we redirect our praise towards children's actions. It's as simple as that.

It's also as *frustratingly simple* as that. It sounds so easy to stop saying 'good girl' and 'clever boy', doesn't it? But it really isn't. Even now, we (the authors) hear ourselves saying 'good girl' to our two daughters and 'good lad' to our son many times a day. But when we say it, how can we take it back? We can't say, 'No, I don't mean that: you're not good!' So the only thing is to follow up any 'intelligence praise' such as 'clever girl' that slips out inadvertently with a process message such as, 'good girl for . . . helping your brother' or '. . . for trying your best to get it right'.

Also, please note that Dweck recommends 'process praise' rather than 'effort praise'. Effort is, of course, important, but it is just one part of the process. Success also comes from determination, strategy, motivation, luck, good coaching, progress and so on. We all know of children who put more effort in than anyone else and yet still don't excel. Similarly, for other children, some new skills seem to come so easily. So don't just emphasise effort. Draw attention to the whole range of processes that go into making progress.

NOW TRY THIS

Review Chapter 1 and Sections 2.1 and 2.2 to see how many links there are between what was recommended there and what you now know of the attitudes and behaviours associated with a growth mindset.

6.7 OTHER WAYS TO BUILD A GROWTH MINDSET

Other recommendations for helping young children get into a growth mindset include the following.

Model a growth mindset

Show your children that you are in a growth mindset. Talk about the progress you are making, the efforts you are putting in, your determination to improve, the hurdles you are overcoming, how inspired you are to learn more and so on. Do this even if you are not in a growth mindset! Fake it if you need to. When you are in a bad mood, you try not to let it affect the children you work with; it is the same with mindset. If you are in a fixed mindset about something, hide it from your children!

Even if you are not in a growth mindset yourself, pretend you are! This will help your children enormously.

Build a growth mindset environment

Check out the messages your learning environment transmits to your children. Does it say: explore, challenge, engage, try? Or does it say play it safe, be careful, do what you can do, be satisfied? The former encourages a growth mindset; the latter transmits fixed mindset messages.

You get what you value

Last year, we welcomed a group of Early Years leaders from Denmark to visit some of our nurseries in Northumberland. Many of them talked about how well organised everything was, how well the children listened to adults, and how well the children behaved. As you can imagine, the host staff were very happy to hear this. They were also a little surprised because, like almost everybody else, they thought their children's behaviour left a lot to be desired!

However, it also left us wondering whether the 'positive' behaviour of the children had come from adults valuing conformity more than exploration, from valuing children doing as they are told rather than developing independence, and from valuing right answers rather than cunning questions! We are not saying that this is necessarily the case, but we are saying that 'we get what we value' and so are therefore asking you: what do you value?

Developing pedagogy

We've lost count of the number of times a leader has shown us around their nursery and, during the tour, has pointed out a few staff who were 'born to work with children'. They've also indicated one or two who they hope will retire or leave very soon! These sorts of comments give the impression that either you've got the knack for pedagogy or you haven't, which is a pretty fixed mindset thing to say. Instead, the growth mindset approach would be to assume we can all improve our pedagogy no matter where we are in our learning journey so far. Those who have already developed a wonderful talent for helping young children flourish can still improve; and those who are less at ease with children can, with the right support and encouragement, begin to learn strategies for improvement. Our pedagogy is on a continuum along which we can all move.

The power of yet

Carol Dweck's TED presentation is well worth watching. It is available on www.TED.com.

(James): In November 2014, I was delighted to arrange for Carol Dweck to make a TED.com presentation in Norrköping, Sweden. At the time of writing, the recording of this ten-minute speech has now been watched 5.5 million times. I assure you the fact that they cut out my introduction before posting the video online does not disappoint me in the slightest. Honestly.

The title of Dweck's presentation that night was 'The Power of Yet'. I notice it has been changed online to 'The Power of Believing That You Can Improve', which is a shame because it is nowhere nearly as catchy or as powerful. Nevertheless, I encourage you to watch it at: www.ted.com/talks/carol_dweck_the_power_of_believing_that_you_can_improve.

In the video, Dweck makes the point very clearly that 'yet' can have a significant effect on attitude. Instead of saying, 'I can't do this', she recommends that we say, 'I can't do this yet'. That three-lettered word changes the possibilities. 'I can't play the guitar yet' implies that I could play the guitar if I put the right effort, time and dedication into it. Saying 'I can't play the guitar' sounds so final.

So, when a child says, 'I can't do it', we recommend that you say, 'Not yet'. This also has the added benefit of acknowledging current reality as well as giving the sense of possibility. Compare this to the common response of saying, 'Yes you can'. Though this might seem just as good, all too often – particularly in cases of low self-esteem – children will respond by thinking either (a) this adult is lying to me or (b) this adult doesn't understand what I'm going through. Then some children will even go as far as to try to prove that they can't do it!

So, instead of saying 'Yes you can', in most cases it would be better to say, 'No you can't yet', as this reflects the child's current reality and then adds a sense of opportunity to improve.

Avoid labelling

(James): I recently noticed a teenager at the back of a maths class who was flailing his arms around frenetically. All the other students were paying full attention to the teacher. This went on for the whole lesson. Afterwards I asked the teacher whether this was normal, to which she replied, rather proudly: 'Damian is a kinaesthetic learner – he learns better when he moves'.

What a load of rubbish! The boy doesn't have a medical condition: he's simply been told he's a kinaesthetic learner and gone along with it because it sounds like fun. His teacher had asked her students to complete a learning styles questionnaire and then concluded that some were visual learners, others were auditory and the rest were kinaesthetic. She'd gone on to declare that visual learners had to see something written down to learn well, auditory learners had to hear something, and the kinaesthetic lot – well, they had to bop and groove to learn!

Don't get me wrong: I agree we all have preferences. I seem to remember things better if I've seen them written down, but it's not impossible for me to learn through listening, despite what my wife would tell you.

However, herein lies a problem: so many people seem to believe that they'll always be good at certain things and therefore never any good at other things, that they tend to steer clear of anything they're not 'naturally' good at. How often, for example, might a father say: 'Don't ask me, I was never any good at spelling – go and ask your mother!' What this implies to the child is: 'Aha, so there's a genetic reason I can't spell: I have a clay-brained father. There's no point in trying because I'll always be bad at spelling'.

Howard Gardner explored this theme at a conference I was also speaking at in 2009 in Kuala Lumpur. He began his keynote speech by saying he wished teachers had never come across his theory of multiple intelligences because so many of them were obsessed with categorising kids. An interesting opening line for a speech attended by more than 1,000 teachers!

Gardner's theory of multiple intelligences proposes that, instead of one general form of intelligence, typically measured by IQ tests, there could be as many as eight intelligences (or nine if you include the existential/spiritual intelligence he has recently been considering):

1 Spatial (ability to visualise)

2 Linguistic (language skills)

3 Logical-mathematical (abstract/logical thought)

4 Bodily-kinaesthetic (dexterity)

5 Interpersonal (understanding others)

6 Intrapersonal (self-awareness)

7 Musical (sensitivity to pitch, rhythm, timbre)

8 Naturalistic (sensitivity to nature)

Multiple Intelligences (Gardner, 1983) is all too often viewed through a fixed mindset lens, whereas the only way in which it can be useful is through a growth mindset lens.

Though responses to Gardner's theory have been mixed, it continues to be used (and misused) in schools around the world. As inspiration for a wider range of activities in lessons, the theory has many benefits. However, using it in the way our friend with a learning styles questionnaire did is nonsensical.

Setting tasks for children based on their horoscope wouldn't be tolerated: strict guidelines for the Capricorns, no rules for the Sagittarians, and plenty of quiet activities for the shy Pisceans. So it has to be wondered why some teachers set tasks according to which of the eight multiple intelligences children have scored most highly on.

Not that adults outside of schools are immune to such silly behaviour. How many times have you heard things said similar to the following in educational settings?

Child: I hate reading books. I can't do it.

Adult: But you're very talented at painting.

(This has the potential to suggest: 'I agree that you're no good at reading, but don't worry about that; you're good at art instead'.)

Adult: Why can't you be more like your sister?

(Message: 'She has talents or attitudes you don't have and probably never will have'.)

Adult: Her brother is the clever one of the family; she's the more social one.

This is problematic because there's a risk of defining and therefore probably predetermining, the skills each child will excel at and which they'll always struggle with.)

The problem with all these example comments is that they imply that skills and talents are fixed. Saying 'never mind about one thing because you'll be more successful with another' suggests that everyone would be better off ignoring their weaknesses and focussing on their strengths. This might be wise advice for job seekers, but early childhood education is not about categorising and defining; it is about exploring, growing, learning, flourishing in all areas of childhood. Isn't it?

6.8 SELF-EFFICACY

Self-efficacy is a measure of how much a person believes he can 'effect' a new outcome. The more self-efficacy a person has, the more influential he believes himself to be.

Self-efficacy is the belief that a person has in his ability to 'effect' or bring about a new outcome. Stanford psychologist Albert Bandura (1977) proposed the term as an alternative to the more widely used term of 'self-esteem'. Whereas the latter relates to how a person 'esteems' or likes her 'self', the idea of self-efficacy relates more to a person's potency and influence. In my mindset, this is what makes self-efficacy the more essential quality (though both would be even better!).

In her meta-analysis on teacher efficacy, Rachel Eells summarises the various work of Albert Bandura (1977–2000), stating: 'Efficacy involves more than positive thinking or optimism. It is tied to the construct of agency (the ability to make things happen) and to action' (2011, p. 5).

Children who are comfortable in their own skin and yet are defeatist when faced with challenges could be said to have high self-esteem but low self-efficacy. Indeed, it is these children who tend to be quickest to shrug their shoulders and say something along the lines of, 'I don't care'. In some circumstances, that might sound reasonable, but what happens when it is actually coming from a fear of failure rather than a genuine disinterest? What if the shoulder shrug is a defence mechanism rather than a show of contentment? This is where self-efficacy comes in. If we help our children to develop their self-efficacy, then they will be more likely to make decisions from a position of aptitude rather than aversion. Knowing they are in a position to 'effect' or create a new outcome *if they wish to* is preferable to avoiding new experiences because of a sense of foreboding or fear.

The beliefs and behaviours associated with low self-efficacy are very similar to those connected to a fixed mindset. Whereas those connected with high self-efficacy match closely to the behaviours of people in a growth mindset.

Figure 57 summarises the differences between low self-efficacy and high self-efficacy.

Incidentally, notice how similar the traits of low self-efficacy are to the behaviours associated with a fixed mindset: both are wary of change; both seem to prefer to prove rather than *improve* themselves; and both are more likely to be frustrated by challenges.

Now compare the similarities in behaviour between those with high self-efficacy and those in a growth mindset. These include having better coping strategies; being open to new situations as well as to change; and choosing growth and expression over playing it safe or showing off to others.

Furthermore, look at the behaviours associated with high self-efficacy, a growth mindset and the traits your children will develop when taking the more challenging path shown in Figure 7 (page 17): resilience, determination, curiosity, being more open to challenges and so on. Again, the links are clear: for our children to develop positive learning attitudes, we need them to also develop high self-efficacy. As John Hattie remarked in his seminal work *Visible Learning*:

> The willingness to invest in learning, to gain a reputation as a learner, and to show openness to experiences are the key dispositional factors that relate to achievement.
>
> (2009, p. 47)

Figure 57: Comparison of low and high self-efficacy

People with **low self-efficacy** tend to be:	People with **high self-efficacy** tend to be:
Rigid in their thinking.	Flexible in their thinking.
Fearful of new and unfamiliar situations.	Keen to experience new situations.
Wary of change.	Open to change.
Cautious of other people.	Cooperative with others.
Keen to prove themselves.	Keen to express themselves.
Reassured by the familiar.	Excited by challenge.
Evasive in what they say.	Honest in what they say.
More likely to give up.	More persistent.
Easily frustrated.	Tolerant.
Less equipped to cope.	Quicker to recover.

6.9 CHAPTER SUMMARY

This chapter has covered the following main points:

1   Progress is synonymous with learning, and, as such, we should do all we can to focus on children's progress rather than on what they can already do.

2   Progress can be shown in many ways, including daily diaries, thinking journals, Progress Trees for reading and Progress Arrows for numeracy.

3   The SOLO Taxonomy is a very useful way to think about progress in learning. SOLO stands for the Structure of the Observed Learning Outcome and was first proposed by John Biggs and Kevin Collis in 1982.

4   The SOLO Taxonomy can help to describe a child's progress from surface-level knowledge to deep understanding.

5   The SOLO Taxonomy links stage for stage with the Learning Challenge that was shared in Sections 2.3–2.7.

6   Helping children get into a growth mindset will help them to flourish and grow.

7   People are in a growth mindset when they believe intelligence and talents are grown and developed rather than innate qualities that we either have or do not have.

8   Praising a child for who they *are* is more likely to put children into a fixed mindset, whereas praising them for what they *do* is more likely to put them into a growth mindset.

9   Self-efficacy has a very important role to play in the lives of our children.

7. FEEDBACK AND LEARNING INTENTIONS

NO ONE ASKS HOW TO MOTIVATE A BABY. A BABY
NATURALLY EXPLORES EVERYTHING IT CAN GET AT, UNLESS
RESTRAINING FORCES HAVE ALREADY BEEN AT WORK. AND
THIS TENDENCY DOESN'T DIE OUT, IT'S WIPED OUT.

(B. F. Skinner, 1948, in his novel *Walden Two*)

7.0 THE IMPACT OF FEEDBACK

Get it right and feedback can significantly improve the quality of learning. Meta-analyses by Hattie, Biggs and Purdie (1996), Black and Wiliam (1998), and Hattie and Jaeger (1998) all cite feedback as one of the most significant factors affecting learning.

Dai Hounsell notes that:

> it has long been recognised, by researchers and practitioners alike, that feedback plays a decisive role in learning and development, within and beyond formal educational settings. We learn faster, and much more effectively, when we have a clear sense of how well we are doing and what we might need to do in order to improve.
>
> (2003, p. 67)

In the 1990s in the UK, one of the most talked-about books amongst teachers and support staff was *Inside the Black Box* by Black and Wiliam (1990). In this thinnest of books, the authors summarised more than 250 research studies, arguing that Assessment for Learning (or AfL, its popular abbreviation) 'could do more to improve educational outcomes than almost any other investment in education' (p. 314).

Sounds good, doesn't it?

However, feedback is not without its pitfalls. When Avraham Kluger and Angelo DeNisi (1996) examined 131 studies involving 12,652 participants in Early Years settings, schools and after-school clubs, they found a *negative* effect in 32% of cases. A full one-third of the effects in those studies showed learners made *less* progress because of the feedback they received!

Is it really that surprising that feedback can be negative though? Think of a time when you were young child making something really nice for one of your parents. Perhaps it was a birthday card or a special picture that you wanted to give them. You put in so much care and attention to making it as lovely as possible. When you gave it to them, you did so with excitement and pride. And then . . . they pointed out your spelling mistakes!

What Kluger and DeNisi found was that if feedback focuses primarily on what children have done wrong, or if it was related to complex tasks that they didn't understand, and/or if it threatened their self-esteem by making them feel as if they couldn't complete the task, then the feedback they received had a negative effect on their learning. Added to this, Kluger and DeNisi also found many types of feedback have next to no effect on learning; this included feedback that included praise for performance and feedback that came with extrinsic rewards.

> Feedback is often quoted as being one of the most significant factors in learning.

> And yet, in one-third of cases, feedback has been shown to have had a negative effect on learning!

> If feedback focusses on what a child has done wrong and leaves her feeling powerless to improve, then it is very likely to have a negative effect on learning.

7.1 WHAT IS FEEDBACK?

Feedback is information that helps to shape the next action.

Feedback is any message – formal or informal, verbal or non-verbal, written or spoken – that helps shape the receiver's next response.

When someone tells a joke, they are looking for feedback; when a child beckons someone over to give advice, he is looking for feedback; if someone touches something too hot, feedback comes in the form of pain; when two microphones amplify each other, the loud squeal is feedback.

Feedback is everywhere. A nod, a wink, a yawn, a point or a cough can all be regarded as feedback.

Though these examples vary in degrees of formality, they all provoke responses: the joker tells another funny story; the child adapts what they are doing; the casualty removes their hand from the heat; and the musician separates the microphones as quickly as possible.

Feedback can come from many different sources: other people, books, games, experiences and self. A child can suggest an alternative strategy to another child; a book can give information that clarifies ideas; a parent can provide encouragement and support; and someone can evaluate his own success.

Winne and Butler (1994) offer an excellent summary in the *International Encyclopaedia of Education*:

> Feedback is information with which a learner can confirm, add to, overwrite, tune, or restructure information in memory, whether that information is domain knowledge, meta-cognitive knowledge, beliefs about self and tasks, or cognitive tactics and strategies.
>
> (p. 5740)

For feedback to be useful to the learning process, it should always answer three questions:

1 What am I trying to achieve?

2 How much progress have I made so far?

3 What should I do next?

Feedback is not just about looking *back*. It is also about looking *forward* and thinking about possible next steps. Some people like to use the term '*feed-forward*'. The problem is that this suggests that feed*back* does not include looking forward – but it does and it should. Indeed, feedback *has* to look forward as well as back if it is to be the hugely powerful influence on learning that research tells us it can be.

Feedback should help your children to answer these three questions:

1 What am I trying to achieve?

2 How much progress have I made so far?

3 What should I do next?

7.2 FEEDBACK AND PRAISE

Praise is not the same as feedback. Feedback answers all three of these questions. Praise, on the other hand, tends only to focus on what children have done well so far.

In their meta-analysis of the effects of feedback on motivation, Edward Deci, Richard Koestner and Richard Ryan (2001) found a *negative* correlation between extrinsic rewards and learning (−0.34). They also found that rewards undermined intrinsic motivation, particularly for interesting tasks (−0.68), although they did find a small positive when the children were engaged in uninteresting tasks (0.18). In other words, extrinsic rewards such as treats or stars on a behaviour chart really work only when tasks are uninspiring. If the activities your children take part in are engaging enough, then they should be their own reward.

That is not to say that praise is a bad thing. Praise might give your children increased confidence to try a task or to stick at it longer. It might also convey a sense of preferred outcome. Indeed, when giving praise, you may well be fulfilling many different roles simultaneously: instructor, trusted adult, guide, encourager, co-explorer, leader, mentor, referee, health and safety officer, and surrogate parent! So, to say that praise is either bad or good would be far too simplistic. Instead, perhaps it is enough to say for now that praise is not always a good thing and that, however much we praise, we ought to keep it separate from feedback. And keep it focussed on actions rather than on the child (as explored in Sections 6.5 and 6.6).

> Praise is not the same as feedback. In fact, praise can reduce the positive effects of feedback.

> That is not to say that praise is a bad thing. Instead, it is to say that praise and feedback should be kept separate from each other.

7.3 LEARNING INTENTIONS AND FEEDBACK

The purpose of Learning Intentions is to give direction to learners and to guide the feedback process so that more progress can be made.

Learning Intentions and Success Criteria should not be viewed simply as a set of instructions to be followed and definitely not as a way to control what is to be learnt. Far too many schools throughout the world have made the mistake of displaying Learning Intentions and Success Criteria at the beginning of lessons and then not referring to them again other than perhaps during a plenary at the end. This is a significant mistake that should not be repeated.

Learning Intentions and Success Criteria *can* be very helpful to the learning process but *only if* the direct link between them and the feedback process is maintained. Break this link, and Learning Intentions become a method by which the authorities setting the curriculum control what the children learn.

Indeed, the link between Learning Intentions, Success Criteria and feedback is so interdependent that there ought not to be one without the other. There should be no Learning Intentions and Success Criteria without feedback and no feedback without Learning Intentions and Success Criteria.

> Learning Intentions and feedback should go hand in hand with each other.

> There should be no Learning Intentions and Success Criteria without feedback and no feedback without Learning Intentions and Success Criteria.

(James): To explain this further, our younger two children, Harry and Phoebe, were playing with LEGOs recently. Harry, aged seven, was building a model by following the instructions carefully. Phoebe, aged three, was using the larger Duplo bricks to create a fantasy world of unicorns and rabbits. Throughout the morning, Harry asked for advice as he built his model, whereas Phoebe asked only that I be a talking horse (apparently, I wasn't expert enough to be a fully fledged unicorn).

As I enjoyed this family time together, a part of me was thinking about feedback opportunities (I was after all, midway through writing this book). The conclusion I came to was that it was going be easier to give Harry feedback than Phoebe. Not because of his age but because he had a clear goal (building the model shown on the box), whereas Phoebe's intentions were more fluid. That didn't make one activity better than the other; it simply made them different.

Harry had a clear goal. That meant we could identify how much progress he had made and what he could do next. We were able to answer the three key feedback questions shown in Section 7.1 together. Phoebe on the other hand, was creating an ever changing fantasy world in which she was writer, director and producer. It wasn't clear what she was trying to achieve, and therefore I had no idea how much progress she was making or what she could do next. This didn't make it any less valuable, of course. Some might even argue that the greater degree of creativity and verbalisation made it a better learning experience than the model building. Personally, I'd be more inclined to say it was 'different' rather than 'better'.

After Harry had finished his model and was looking for something else to do, I suggested they play together. Phoebe wasn't sure Harry could handle being a horse, never mind a unicorn, so we thought about alternatives. After a few proposals were dismissed, they settled on a modelling competition. One of them would build something with the Duplo bricks, and the other one would try to copy it.

Phoebe started by putting four bricks together to build a farmhouse (for unicorns, of course). Harry copied and got it right the first time.

Harry then built a tower with a pattern of alternating colours: red brick, white brick, red brick, white brick and so on. Phoebe built a similar structure. However, it wasn't *exactly* the same: hers had random colours and was one brick shorter than Harry's.

Now there was the opportunity for feedback because there was a clear goal, and therefore we could start on with the three feedback questions. We had agreed that Phoebe would build exactly the same model as her brother. This meant we could also think about how much progress she'd made so far and what she could do next. And so the game continued: each child building models with increasing complexity for the other to replicate. Even I got to join in until I naively tried to build a unicorn and was banned from further participation.

Interestingly enough, Phoebe showed a greater sense of achievement in this 'replicating' game than she had for her original, fantasy game. That is not to say she enjoyed it more, just that she felt a great sense of accomplishment.

NOW TRY THIS

To illustrate this point further, please try the following activity. It is something that I often use when making keynote speeches at conferences. To begin with, I ask delegates to draw a house. I give them 45 seconds to do so. Why not try it now yourself?

7.3.1 Draw a house!

Draw a house here!

Once the 45 seconds are over, I then ask delegates to give each other feedback about their houses.

If you were to give yourself feedback about your house, what would you say? Write your suggestions here.

7.3.2 Generate feedback about your house!

7.3.3 Improve your house!

Using the brilliant feedback you've just given yourself, now improve your house! Take no more than 20 seconds to do so. If you have a different colour pen, then use that to make your edits. This will help you to track the changes if and when you look back at these pages sometime in the future.

Give yourself some feedback about your house (or ask a friend to give you some feedback).

Now use your feedback to improve your house.

7.3.4 Review of the house-drawing exercise

Looking at the feedback you generated about your house, how useful was it? Did the quality of the finished drawing improve as a result of your feedback? If your feedback was of high quality, then your drawing certainly should have improved.

But we bet your feedback wasn't high quality. And, therefore, we bet your house did *not* improve as a result of your feedback.

Please don't be offended! We are not saying you *can't* give high-quality feedback. We are simply saying you *couldn't* give high-quality feedback in this *particular* task.

We prevented you from generating high-quality feedback because we gave no other instructions than 'draw a house'. We did not explain what *kind* of house, nor did we identify the features needed in this particular activity. In some ways, of course, that makes things easier for you: it means you can draw *any* house and be happy with it.

However, it also makes things much harder for you because it stops you from generating useful feedback. Without clear criteria for success, the only way you could have answered the three key feedback questions (see Section 7.1) would have been along the lines of the answers shown in brackets here:

> 1   What am I trying to achieve? **(I'm drawing a house!)**
>
> 2   How much progress have I made so far? **(There's my house.)**
>
> 3   What should I do next? **(Finish it.)**

Compare this to a different scenario in which we had set up the task this way instead:

> We'd like you to draw a house. The following features should be included:

> • Between four and six windows (at least one of which is open)
>
> • A front door
>
> • Somewhere to post letters
>
> • A sloping roof
>
> • Signs of life

Now think about the feedback you could have given yourself after you'd finished your initial drawing! It would probably have been more like the answers shown in brackets in the following examples:

> 1   What am I trying to achieve? **(I'm drawing a house with five windows, a front door, a letter box, a sloping roof and some signs of life.)**
>
> 2   How much progress have I made so far? **(I've drawn the windows, door, letter box and roof.)**
>
> 3   What should I do next? **(I need to add some signs of life. I'm thinking perhaps a cat in the window, a dog kennel in the garden and some kids' toys lying around outside.)**

Compare the difference in quality between the answers in brackets in the first example and the answers in brackets in this second example. *That* is why we would go as far as to say that if your children do not know the (learning) goal, then do not give them feedback. By all means encourage them and engage with them, but do not give them feedback unless you first agree on a goal together.

7.3.5 This does not kill creativity!

When we use this sort of example at conferences, some people worry about the effect on creativity. They start to wonder whether we are advocating a 'painting by numbers' approach to learning. The quick answer to this is no, we are not trying to kill creativity!

To calm any nerves, here is the way we should have introduced the task to you:

> I would like you to draw a house please. Any shape, any size and any style of architecture. You choose what type of dwelling – be it a giant's castle, a hobbit hole or a two-up, two-down semi by the sea. The features we are looking for today are four–six windows (any shape, any size, any location), a front door (doesn't have to be on the ground floor), somewhere to post letters (doesn't have to be a letterbox in the front door – perhaps it could be a hole in the roof for the giant postman), a sloping roof and some signs of life. These are not the only features of a house, and you certainly would not see them on every house. But they are what we are looking for *today*. And more importantly – they are the features that I would like you to look for when giving each other feedback after you've all finished draft one.

Introducing the task in this way would clarify the goals and therefore make it much more likely that you can give yourself and others useful feedback. It should not hamper their imagination or individual flair.

7.4 TIMING

Feedback should be part of the learning process for your children. It does not work as well if it is offered after the learning activity is over. Think of teaching a child to ride a bike: none of us would wait until they'd finished before telling them how to do it better! We would give feedback in the moment. We would watch how well they got on initially, and then we'd offer feedback on how to improve so that they could test out the suggestions straightaway. In other words, we would answer the three feedback questions during the learning activity rather than wait until it is over.

Of course, this seems to be plain old common sense, and yet it is just not that common. Think of how many children in school receive feedback from their teachers *after* they've completed their work! They are asked to write a story, paint a picture, do some group work, and then afterwards their teacher tells them how they could have done it better if only they had thought of that whilst they were doing it. Crazy, eh? This is why we've created the Seven Steps to Feedback Success, showing that our feedback should come at Step Five, not Step Seven. See Section 7.7 for more information.

Feedback should be part of the learning process for your children. It does not work as well if it is offered after the learning activity is over

7.5 SITTING BESIDE YOUR CHILDREN

The English word 'assessment' has its roots in the Latin verb *assidere*, meaning 'to sit beside'. This 'sitting beside' form of feedback is the best way to engage your children in the feedback process. It makes feedback more collaborative and constructive. By 'sitting beside' your children (whether literally or metaphorically), you should be able to better understand what and why they've done what they've done so far and what they might be able to do to improve. Perhaps more importantly, this 'sitting beside' should also enable and encourage your children to think of answers to the three feedback questions themselves rather than to rely on your spoon-feeding them some options.

'Assessment' has its roots in the Latin verb assidere, meaning 'to sit beside'.

The sorts of questions we might ask ourselves and our children whilst 'sitting beside' each other include:

1. Do they understand what they are trying to achieve?

This would usually include finding out:

- What do they think the Learning Intentions are?
- Do these Learning Intentions seem interesting?
- What steps do they think they need to take in order to reach their Learning Intention?
- Which steps are going to be the most challenging?
- Are there any steps they think will be too easy?

Some of the questions to ask when 'sitting beside' children include:

1 What are they trying to do?

2 How well do they think they have done well so far?

3 What could they do next to make things even better?

2. How much progress do they think they've made already?

It would be good to find out what your children think of the following:

- How much progress do they think they've made so far?

- How 'far' from their Learning Intention are they at the moment?

- How satisfied are they with the steps they've already taken?

- Are there any steps they think they've overlooked?

- What else were they going to do but haven't done already?

3. What could they do next?

The following questions should help your children identify for themselves what they might do next:

- What else could you do to make it work even better?

- Is there anything you've already done that you could do even better?

- What has someone else done that you could also do now?

- How hard do you think you've tried so far?

- What could you do to make it even more fun/interesting/challenging?

Things to notice about these questions

Education comes from the Latin verb *educere*, meaning 'to draw out'. This fits nicely with these questions and with the process of *sitting beside* our children to draw out their ideas and understanding.

Asking your children what *they* think rather than telling them what to do next should, over time, help them to become more capable learners.

7.6 ENCOURAGING THE RIGHT TYPE OF FEEDBACK

All the ideas we've covered so far will work brilliantly only if they are part of a positive feedback culture. To create such an ethos, we encourage you to think about the following aspects of learning.

7.6.1 Build safety and trust

Safety and trust should be at the heart of feedback. Without these, none – or at least very few – of the characteristics described in this section are likely to work. As Alan E Beck (1994) put it: 'You can't do the Bloom stuff until you take care of the Maslow stuff'.

Safety and trust should be at the heart of feedback.

Of course, we can't control all the influences that impinge on a young child's sense of safety and well-being. However, we can do many things to use feedback to help build an atmosphere of trust and intellectual safety. These include:

> **Be transparent**: Ensure that feedback relates to clear Learning Intentions. Your children should know what goals they are aiming for if feedback is going to be anything other than an unwelcome surprise. Remember the story in Section 7.0 of one of your parents correcting your spelling mistakes after you had made them a lovely birthday card!

> **Be equitable**: All children benefit from high quality, well timed feedback. Try not to focus your attentions too much on some children at the expense of others. Even the most capable children can learn lots from feedback.

> **Be nice**: Children learn more from people they like. So be a likeable person! Treat children with respect, offer positive reinforcement, smile, listen, show an interest in their interests and greet every child by name. In other words, show that you care *for* them and *about* them.

Be consistent: Agree on the Learning Intentions beforehand, and then ensure that the feedback you offer focuses on these goals. Avoid inconsistencies such as referencing Learning Intentions with some children whilst offering unrelated feedback to others.

Personalise feedback . . .: Get to know your children as well as you can. What motivates them? How confident are they? What makes them tick? Once you know answers to these questions, tailor feedback accordingly so that every child is encouraged to learn and grow.

. . . without being personal: Feedback should relate to actions rather than to the person. As explored in Sections 6.4–6.8, feedback that is directed towards the qualities of a child (even if those qualities are positive) can have a negative effect on learning. So always focus feedback on outcomes, actions or ideas.

7.6.2 Reframe feedback as clues for learning

Too many people believe feedback is a judgement *about them*. This makes feedback that is negative (or feels negative) as unwelcome as a mosquito bite.

If we can frame feedback as information to learn from, then the giving and receiving of feedback becomes far less threatening.

Another way to think about it is to reimagine feedback as the revealing of clues with which to solve a mystery or reach a goal. This makes the whole process much more desirable.

It is useful to imagine feedback as the revealing of clues with which to solve a mystery or reach a goal.

So, when you set Learning Intentions with your children, try presenting them as if they are the 'X' marking the spot on a treasure map. Create a sense of desire to reach X by outlining the benefits. Invite clarifying and thought-provoking questions to build your children's appetite for the learning journey. Say that you are really looking forward to finding out what they will learn along the way.

Once that's all set up – and, of course, that won't happen overnight – then it will be much easier to reframe feedback as clues to help children on their learning journey. In such an atmosphere, your children will be as keen as mustard to uncover the next clue. And if you remind them that it is in everyone's interest to get as many children closer to X as possible, then they should be even keener to work together to uncover the 'secrets'.

Of course, this sounds all very idealistic, but if we can move *towards* this scenario, then imagine the effect it could have on your children's learning! Rather than feedback being viewed as necessary criticism, it could be viewed as a desirable advantage; instead of being avoided unless absolutely necessary, it could be sought out whenever the opportunity presents itself; and instead of being thought of as a judgement at the end, it could be thought of as ideas for learning even more.

7.6.3 Design for eureka moments

Children are more likely to seek out and welcome feedback when they are engaged in activities that lead to a eureka moment. A eureka moment is when someone feels a sense of revelation. It is when she believes she has figured it out for herself.

Children are more likely to seek out and welcome feedback when they are in search of a mystery or revelation.

Coming from the Greek for 'I found it', eureka moments are exactly that: 'I found it. My teacher didn't give me the answer. My friend didn't show me how to do it. I discovered it for myself. I figured it out, and I feel great'.

The key to eureka is that the feelings are generated only when children have had to struggle to reach an understanding. In other words, they will need to go through the Learning Pit (see Sections 2.3 and 2.5). If your children do not engage in challenging tasks, then they will have no chance of reaching their eureka moments. If success has come too easily for them, then they may well feel a sense of relief at having 'finished', but they will not experience the elation of eureka.

Eureka feels great. So once your children experience eureka, they will want to repeat it again and again. This will lead to an increased willingness to engage in challenging tasks – which in turn will lead to a greater desire for feedback since it is when children are engaged in demanding tasks that will want more feedback.

Increase the challenge, and you will increase your children's desire for feedback!

7.6.4 Keep half an eye on brain research

In recent years, there has been an explosion of theories about how people learn. Exciting discoveries in neuroscience and continued developments in cognitive psychology have presented new ways of thinking about the brain. Explanations of how the brain works have used metaphors varying from computers that process information, create, store and manipulate data to a jungle with its layered world of interwoven, interdependent neurological connections.

However, we should be careful about how we link current research with how the brain works, particularly if we then make recommendations about specific approaches to learning. Scientists caution that the brain is complex, and, although research has revealed some significant findings, there is no widespread agreement about their applicability to education.

That said, there seems to be general agreement about the following:

- Activities that are stimulating and challenging are more likely to pass through the reticular activating system (a filter in the lower brain that focuses attention on novel changes perceived in the environment).

- Experiences that are free of intimidation may help information pass through the amygdala's affective filter.

- When learning is pleasurable, the brain releases dopamine, a neurotransmitter that stimulates the memory centres and promotes the release of acetylcholine that in turn increases focussed attention.

If these early findings are accurate, then perhaps we can also assume that feedback will flourish under similar conditions; that is to say, feedback is improved when it is stimulating, challenging and free from intimidation.

7.6.5 Walk the talk

Everyone involved in learning should walk the talk – including the adults. As the saying goes, 'Children are great imitators so give them something great to imitate'.

To be the embodiment of a great feedback culture, we should share with our children that:

- We often make mistakes.

- We believe mistakes are a normal part of learning.

- We don't have all the answers.

- We look to others for support and guidance.

- We welcome feedback as part of our learning journey.

- We examine our mistakes as a way to learn most from them.

- We are always trying to improve the way in which we give, receive and act upon feedback.

7.6.6 Share the culture

Feedback should be a constructive conversation about a child's progress towards an agreed goal. It should never be given – or perceived as – personal criticism.

To increase the likelihood of this becoming a reality, make sure you share with everyone – colleagues, children and their parents – what type of feedback culture you are aiming to engender. Engage everyone in creating and promoting the culture. Help them to know what they should expect an excellent feedback culture to feel like, sound like and look like.

As part of this, be open to a 360-degree process of feedback. This means inviting, valuing and responding to feedback from colleagues, managers, children and yourself; in other words, from everyone around you – hence the term '360 degrees'. This is in contrast to the more common forms of feedback that come from manager to employee or from adult to child.

Remember that feedback is often influenced by the prevailing learning culture and not just by the relationship between the individuals giving and receiving the feedback. So pay close attention to the learning culture and ensure you do all you can to build and share the positive aspects of that culture.

7.6.7 Keep feedback flowing

Feedback should be ongoing, familiar and expected. It should not be something that takes your children by surprise or something that unnerves them. So keep the feedback flowing! And we don't just mean from you to them but also from them to you and from them to one another.

Also remember that feedback is much more effective when it is regular, cumulative and developmental rather than random and unconnected. By being regular, your children will be more able to anticipate and respond to feedback. By being cumulative, feedback will help your children to build on their prior learning and take ever more steps towards their Learning Intentions. And by being developmental, feedback will help your children to improve and grow their learning abilities.

7.7 SEVEN STEPS TO FEEDBACK SUCCESS

Please consider the previous six sections as the warm-up to this section! Indeed, everything that has gone before in this chapter has prepared the ground and given the justification for the Seven Steps to Feedback Success.

But before we start, here is one more thought: if, as so much research has shown, feedback can double the amount of progress children make, then why isn't every child making huge strides in their learning? Surely every adult is giving every child feedback every day, so how come the effect of that feedback is nowhere near as great as the evidence suggests it could be?

Either the research is wrong, or adults aren't really giving children as much feedback as they say they are? Or more likely, it is because we're not quite using feedback as effectively as we could.

That is what has prompted the Seven Steps to Feedback Success: to help all of us give feedback that is so effective that it helps *all* children make superb progress in their learning.

Here are the Seven Steps to Feedback Success:

1   Agree on Learning Intentions

2   First goes

3   Review

4   Improve

5   Teacher feedback

6   Improve again

7   Reflect*

7.7.1 Agree on Learning Intentions

Start the Seven Steps to Feedback Success by agreeing on some Learning Intentions. If your children don't understand what they are trying to do, then feedback is not really going to work very well. Remember how much better your feedback to yourself and to others could have been in the 'Draw a house' exercise in Section 7.3.1 if you had known the criteria for success beforehand.

Example early Learning Intentions would include:

- We are learning to paint a picture of something we have seen today. To be successful, we will also think about (1) using the whole page and (2) mixing paints so that we use at least three colours in our picture.

- We are learning to wash our hands properly by remembering to (1) pull up our sleeves first, (2) turn on the tap and wet our hands, (3) put on some soap on and rub our hands and fingers together, (4) wash the soap off under the water, (5) dry our hands properly.

Feedback should be ongoing, familiar and expected. It should not be something that takes your children by surprise or something that unnerves them.

The best way to ensure that feedback works every time is to follow the Seven Steps to Feedback Success.

The Seven Steps to Feedback Success should always begin with agreeing on the Learning Intentions. Without this agreement, feedback is unlikely to work well.

- We are learning how to plant some seeds by remembering to (1) putting soil into a plant pot, (2) sprinkling some seeds on the soil, (3) carefully pushing the seeds into the soil, (4) watering the soil gently, (5) putting the pot on the windowsill so that it gets some sunlight.

- We are learning about money by thinking about (1) what to buy in our play shop, (2) asking how much it costs, (3) counting out the right number of coins.

- We are practising our throwing by (1) looking at the hoop we are aiming for, (2) throwing a beanbag underarm towards the hoop, (3) changing how hard we throw the beanbag each time to make sure it lands inside the hoop.

In these examples, please notice the following:

1 A Learning Intention is followed by some Success Criteria (numbered for your ease of reference).

2 Each goal is described as a Learning Intention rather than simply as an action. For example, 'We are learning how to plant' rather than 'We are planting'.

3 We have used the phrase, 'By remembering to'. This is a good way to introduce Success Criteria to young children.

The activity ideas in Chapter 8 give other examples of Learning Intentions and Success Criteria.

7.7.2 First goes

Once your children understand the goals (Learning Intentions) and what they should do to make progress (Success Criteria), then they ought to be ready to begin.

If their learning involves producing something, then encourage them to say they are creating their 'first draft' or 'first version' rather than 'doing it'. Similarly, if they are performing something (e.g. a physical skill), then get them to talk in terms of their 'first go' rather than their 'doing it'. The differences might seem subtle, but they can be significant.

> 'First draft' implies that there will be some editing to follow. It is the same with 'first go' – there is the inference that adjustments will be made.

'First draft' implies that there will be some editing to follow. It is the same with 'first go' – there is the inference that adjustments will be made. Whereas if your children talk about 'doing their work' or 'doing it', then they might think that (a) if it doesn't work, then they are a failure or (b) after they've done it once, then there is nothing more to be done. In both these cases, learning is likely to be constrained by the lack of revisions and edits.

7.7.3 Review

After your children have had a few goes, encourage them to stop and think about how well they are doing so far. Make sure they think about the Success Criteria and compare their performance against those criteria rather than against the actions of others. So instead of saying, 'I am doing better or worse than my friend', they should think about which criteria they have succeeded at and which ones they have yet to do.

> Self and peer feedback is a vital step in helping your children to understand the process of learning.

Self and peer feedback are vital steps in helping your children to understand the process of learning. Resist the urge to offer your insights at this stage. Encourage – and perhaps support – but do not lead this stage of the feedback process. Let your children develop their independent learning strategies.

Remind your children that they will be able to generate useful feedback for themselves and for one another if they follow these steps:

1 Think about what you are learning and the steps that will get you there. For example, we are learning about matching colours by remembering to put objects of the same colour together.

2 Now compare your first attempts against these goals. Which criteria have you done really well with and which ones could you improve?

3 Based on your answers to these questions, think of all the things you could do so that you get even closer to your Learning Intention next time.

In summary, you are encouraging your children to answer the three feedback questions:

1 What are we learning?

2 How well have we done so far?

3 What could we do next?

Remind your children to answer all three questions when giving themselves or others feedback.

7.7.4 Improve

Based on the feedback they have given themselves or one another, your children can now improve what they have done so far. This does *not* mean that they should re-do the whole thing! Instead, they should make additions and corrections.

7.7.5 Teacher feedback

Only once your children have completed Stages 1–4 is it time for some teacher-led (or other-adult-led) feedback. Of course, you might have been giving encouragement throughout the process but Stage 5 of the Seven Steps to Feedback Success is the time to give your more formal feedback.

Only once your children have completed Stages 1–4 is it time for adult-led feedback.

Many conventions are popular in Early Years and primary education – such as Three Stars and a Wish – but many of these are built on the belief that children need to hear lots of positive messages for every 'negative' comment. As we hope you will have understood from reading this book, feedback should not be viewed in terms of being negative or positive. Of course, feedback generally *is* viewed in these terms, but that doesn't mean that it *should* be!

So long as you get the feedback culture right such that your children (and the adults) view feedback as information (neither good nor bad) that can be used to make progress, then the best kind of feedback consists of advice and suggestions. Not a little bit of 'negative stuff' mixed in with lots of positives. It should be advice, advice, advice!

Advice would include ideas about what could be changed, amended, left alone, added to or scrapped altogether. And it should always be focussed on the task or the process, not on the children themselves. For example, 'Try bending your elbow more when you throw the beanbag' rather than 'You are a good thrower; keep going!' For more about avoiding child-focussed feedback, see Sections 6.5, 6.6 and 7.2.

When giving feedback to your children, think of yourself as a coach rather than a referee. You are not there just to reward or penalise; you are there to guide, challenge, encourage and stretch.

Also, please remember that, when giving feedback, you should be less of a referee and more of a coach (Figure 58).

Figure 58: Coach or referee?

If we were to say that a referee adjudicates and decides whereas a coach supports, challenges, trains, stretches and instructs, then it is very obvious that our role in education is closer to that of a coach. Of course, sometimes we should be the referee (when supervising a competitive game, for example). But most of the time, we should be the coach. That is assuming we want to help our children make more progress rather than simply check what they are able to do!

Sticking with the analogy of a coach, consider the similarities between what an excellent coach might do and what you might do as a teacher:

An excellent coach would:

1 Welcome the team and engage the players in an enjoyable warm-up (for example, for non-sporty activities, this might be a brain teaser or stimulus for thinking).

2 Give them a clear sense of the focus for the session (identify the Learning Intentions).

3 Ask for suggestions about how they will achieve the Learning Intention or give the players a clear set of instructions (this is identifying the Success Criteria).

4 Invite a more proficient performer (perhaps from another team) to demonstrate the skill.

5 Give the players time to experiment and try out the skills (first goes).

6 Circulate around the players, giving individualised attention including encouragement and additional challenges.

7 Split the players into groups and ask them to give one another feedback about how to improve the skills they are currently working on (self/peer review).

8 Give more time to practise (improve).

9 Offer expert guidance on how to improve. Those players who have met or exceeded the target would be given additional challenges or be asked to apply the skills in a game; those who are nearly there would be asked to keep working on the final bits of the skill; and those who are a long way off would be given some support so that they feel as if the session has not been entirely wasted and that they have made some progress.

10 Most training sessions would then finish off with a game in which all players would be expected to try out their new skills (reiterating context and purpose).

Compare this to an excellent referee, who would:

1 Remind the players to play fair.

2 Enforce the rules of the game.

3 Act as timekeeper.

4 Punish serious offences.

5 Keep the game flowing as much as possible.

6 Provide the appropriate authorities with a match report.

7 Ensure the safety of the players.

Of course, early childhood education *is* different from the world of sport. But there are many parallels. And hopefully by sharing this perhaps overworked example, we hope we've drawn attention to how much more powerful feedback can be when you think of yourself as the coach rather than the referee!

Stick to the point

As you review your children's work, make sure you refer all feedback back to the Learning Intentions and Success Criteria. Do not veer off into territory that your children have not anticipated.

For example, if the Learning Intention and Success Criteria were to build a tower from blocks, making sure that there are five or more bricks and that they are stacked one on top of the other, then resist the temptation to give feedback about something else. It might seem perfectly OK to comment on a child's choice of brick colours or to praise one child for building the tallest tower, but this is unfair to the other children who will quite rightly feel as if the task is less about

When giving feedback, always refer to the Learning Intentions and Success Criteria. Do not veer off into territory that your children have not anticipated.

achieving the Success Criteria and more about pleasing the adult. If this happens too often, then your children are very likely to grow mistrustful of feedback and think some feedback is complimentary and other feedback is criticism. Instead, it is much healthier to think of feedback purely as information with which to make more progress (as described in Section 7.6.2).

7.7.6 Improve again

Now your children should have their final goes or make amendments to whatever they are making. They have had their first goes; reviewed it themselves or with one another; improved it and then received advice from you. So now they are ready to make their final adjustments.

It is frankly baffling how many learners have to wait until *after* they've finished before an adult gives them feedback. Why does this happen? If ever there was a case of closing the stable door after the horse has bolted, then this is it.

Of course, many teachers will make comments such as, 'The next time you do that, don't forget to do *x*, *y* and *z*'. But unless your children have got a much better memory than most, the chances are they will not remember your advice the next time they have a go at something similar.

And yet so very many teachers have asked us: 'Isn't it cheating to let kids improve their work after you've shown them what to do?' Ummm, no! That would be confusing 'cheating' with 'teaching'! 'But won't they do better after your feedback?' they retort. 'We certainly hope so; otherwise what on earth is the point of feedback?!' Remember: we are there to coach, support, guide and encourage, not just to supervise and penalise.

7.7.7 Reflect*

In the Seven Steps to Feedback Success for school-aged students, this step is identified as an optional step for grading. That is why we've put an asterisk next to the heading because of the change in activity for younger children.

The final stage in the Seven Steps is to encourage your children to think back over their learning and to identify what they have done well, what they have enjoyed most, what they have learnt and what they might do differently next time.

We have given guidance for some of the best ways to lead children in this process in Stage 4 of each of the activities in Chapter 8.

7.8 THE SEVEN STEPS TO FEEDBACK SUCCESS: SOME FINAL THOUGHTS

Some years ago, it was commonplace for leaders to watch teachers *teach*. This is the wrong emphasis: why focus on the teaching when it's the *learning* that matters most? Far too often, teaching doesn't lead to the intended learning – and sometimes even gets in the way of learning. Whereas at other times, the best learning takes place when there is no teaching!

Thankfully, things have moved on since then, and now it is far more commonplace for leaders to observe learning (often asking children the three key feedback questions. What are you learning? How well are you doing so far? What could you do next?). However, the profession doesn't seem to have moved on so quickly when it comes to feedback: many people are still looking at the feedback itself rather than the *effect* of the feedback.

So let's be clear: the quality of feedback should be judged not on what is transmitted but on what is understood and used to good effect by the learner.

In the same way that teaching is the transmission of information and learning is the receiving and application of that information, so feedback is the transmission of information, and the 'effect' is the receiving and applying of that information. So, just as we moved on from judging the quality of *teaching* and started now to look more at the quality of *learning*, so we should now also be moving on from looking at the quality of *feedback* to looking at the quality of the *effect* of feedback.

Once you have given your children feedback, then they should make their final adjustments or have their final goes. This increases the likelihood of feedback having the impact that research tells us it should.

Feedback should not be judged according to how or what advice is given. Instead, it should be judged in terms of the effect it has on the children's learning.

Why so many schools insist on having 'marking policies' showing how to mark and when to mark is baffling. Surely it would be better to create Learning from Feedback policies that seek to examine the *impact* of feedback on learners' progress? So it should be for all young learners. Let's not monitor on the quality of feedback *given*; instead, let's think about the *effect* of feedback on our young learners. Is it helping them to grow in confidence and ability? Is it helping them to make more progress and to engage in even deeper learning? Or is it simply being used as a way to correct and control?

7.9 CHAPTER SUMMARY

This chapter has covered the following main points:

1   The Seven Steps to Feedback Success brings together all the best research, theory and practice available to maximise the possibility of feedback working brilliantly.

2   Research from many sources, including John Hattie and Dylan Wiliam, identifies feedback as one of the most significant factors in learning, saying it often leads to a doubling of the normal rate of student progress.

3   Most adults are already giving feedback to their children, but most children are not achieving anything like double the normal rate of progress.

4   Adults must therefore be doing things that are ineffective. Or there are effective things that adults are not doing (yet). The Seven Steps to Feedback Success aims to redress the balance.

5   Key aspects of the Seven Steps include teaching your children how to give themselves and one another feedback.

6   Ensure that feedback corresponds to the agreed Learning Intentions and Success Criteria.

7   Give your feedback *before* your children finish the activity, not *after* it.

8   Get the feedback culture right, and use the Seven Steps properly; *then* you will see the sort of impact that Hattie, Wiliam et al. are promising!

8 EARLY LEARNING ACTIVITIES

This final chapter shares some excellent examples for engaging young children in activities that will help them to learn how to learn.

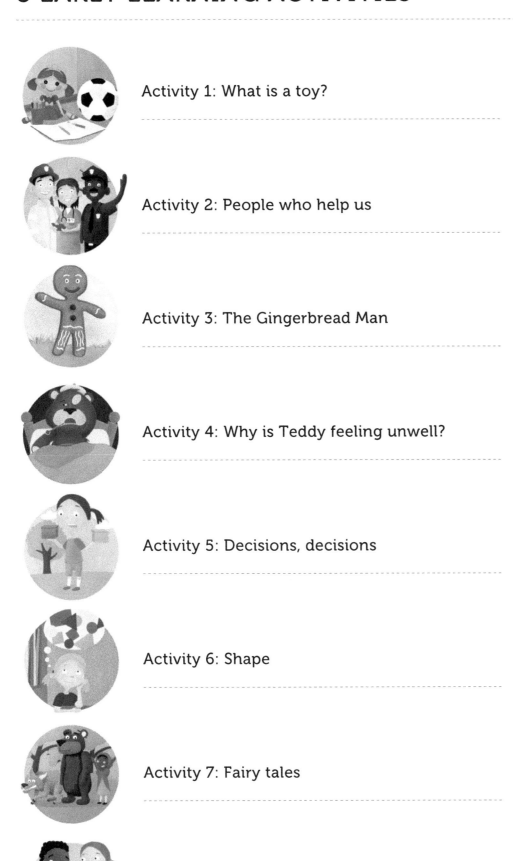

Activity 1: What is a toy?

Activity 2: People who help us

Activity 3: The Gingerbread Man

Activity 4: Why is Teddy feeling unwell?

Activity 5: Decisions, decisions

Activity 6: Shape

Activity 7: Fairy tales

Activity 8: Being a good friend

Activity 1:

What is a toy?

Young children are often encouraged to 'go and play with your toys', but what is meant by 'toy'? Is it *anything* that can be played with (e.g. sticks and stones) or only things that are *intended* to be played with (e.g. dolls)? This also has safety implications; for example, should children play with sharp objects? Should toys always be safe?

KEY CONCEPT

Toys

KEY WORDS

Toy, play, game, fun, enjoy, imagination, role play, construction, art, creativity, comfort, activity, exercise

LEARNING INTENTION

To understand what makes something a toy

SUCCESS CRITERIA

We can:

- Talk about our own toys and what they mean to us.
- Decide which objects are toys and which are not.
- Explain what makes something a toy.
- Identify things that a toy *must* have or do.
- Identify things that toys do *not* need to have or do.

STRATEGIES USED

Sorting and Classifying

Concept Line

Odd One Out

1. IDENTIFY IMPORTANT CONCEPTS

Toys come in all shapes and sizes and form an important part of childhood and development.

Support discussion around what makes something a toy and what the purpose and role of toys are. The children's ideas should be challenged for reasons, and you should use both general and specific examples to test the ideas and reasons generated.

Areas of exploration can include examples of toys in different ages, different contexts and a variety of cultural environments.

Key questions to consider include:

- What makes something a toy?
- When does something stop being a toy?
- What do all toys have in common?

2. CHALLENGE CHILDREN'S UNDERSTANDING

Figure 59 presents some examples of cognitive conflict we expect your children to experience.

Figure 59: Cognitive conflict about toys

Opinion	Conflicting opinion
A toy is something you play with.	My mum says I play with my food.
Toys are for children	My dad's phone has great games on it.
Suzy says dolls are for girls to play with.	I like playing with dolls, and I am a boy.

Create challenge using some of these questions:

- What is a toy?
- Why do we like toys?
- How do toys make us feel?
- What is your favourite toy?
- Can something be a toy if has never been played with?
- Can you play with something and it not be a toy?
- Are all toys play things?
- Are toys only for children?
- Can pets or friends be toys?
- Can we play without any toys?
- How important is it that shops make different toys for boys and girls?

- Does a toy have to be an object?
- Can anything be a toy?
- Are musical instruments toys?
- What would life be like without toys?
- At what age should we stop playing with toys?

3. CONSTRUCT UNDERSTANDING

Help your children make sense of their thoughts using one or more of the following activities.

Activity 1: Sorting and Classifying

Sit in a circle with your children, and explain that there has been a mix-up, and you need some help in sorting out all the 'toys' from the 'non-toys' in the box. You can present the children with a bag or box full of objects (based on the activity cards or other objects) or use the activity cards supplied in Figure 62 (page 133).

Remind your children of the ideas that came out of the discussion during the cognitive conflict stage. Then invite individuals to choose an object or card from the bag/box and describe it to the other children. They should then say whether they think it is a toy or not and be encouraged to give reasons for their answers. The other children can say whether they agree or disagree with the classification and why.

Encourage your children to listen and respond to different reasons given and move towards a group decision before it is put into either the 'toy' category or the 'non-toy' category. The respective categories can be represented by two circles on the floor either drawn out or created by hoops or rope.

Always encourage your children to justify their decisions and ideas with reasoning:

- Why do you think that is a toy?
- Is that the only reason why that is a toy?
- Is that the most important reason for it being a toy?
- Does everyone agree?
- Does anyone disagree?
- Does anyone think that there is a different reason for why it is a toy that is more important than this one?
- Are there any cards/objects that you feel are definitely not toys?
- How can you tell whether something is not a toy?

Your children can sort the cards/objects in different ways as the discussion progresses.

- 'Toy', 'not a toy', 'not sure', 'not normally a toy but could be'
- Make links between cards/objects and common criteria (e.g. bounces, makes a noise, role play, fun, comforting)
- Human-made toy, natural toy, imaginary toy

Support your children to think about the sorting criteria as they place the cards/objects into groups. For example, if they decide being a 'toy' means 'it has to be something you can play with', then all cards/objects relating to this should go into one pile and other clues that do not fit this criterion should go into another pile.

Figure 60: Concept Line for toys

Activity 2: Concept Line

Alternatively, they can place the cards on a continuum or Concept Line (line of rope or string) with the most definite example of a toy at one end and the least likely to be a toy at the other end. They can then place all the other objects/cards at a suitable place along the line to represent how much of a toy or non-toy it is. (See Figure 60.)

EXTENSION/SIMPLIFICATION

To extend the learning further, you could ask your children to think of other examples that could be included in the sorting process. Each time they think of a new object, encourage them to use it to test their ideas. These questions should help:

- Does this fit the description of a toy?
- Does it have anything else about it that makes it a toy that we have not considered yet?
- In what ways might this not be a toy?
- Do all toys need to share the same characteristics as this one?

Activity 3: Odd One Out

To simplify the task, you could give your children fewer cards or objects to consider. You could also use the Odd One Out strategy to ask them to compare just three examples rather than sharing all the objects with them. (See Figure 61.) For example:

Figure 61: Odd One Out of a teddy, a kitten and a doll

4. CONSIDER THE LEARNING JOURNEY

Ask your children to consider how they came to their decision and about the process they went through to get there. Questions such as these could help:

- How did you make your decision?

- Is it important to agree on an answer together?

- What helped you to decide?

- If you could not have reached a decision, what could you have done next?

Transfer activity ideas:

- Each child could become a toy detective and investigate the school, grounds and home to find as many examples of toys or potential toys as possible. These can be recorded as drawings or photographs.

- Each child could bring his favourite toy into school and do a show-and-tell about what makes that toy their favourite.

- Each child could bring in an object that can be played with but that would not normally be thought of as a toy.

- Your children could engage in an art activity to design the perfect toy for an alien from another planet who had never had a toy before.

Figure 62: Activity Cards: 'What is a toy?'

ACTIVITY:
What is a toy?
1-4
A bed sheet

©2017 www.challenginglearning.com

ACTIVITY:
What is a toy?
1-5
A treasure chest

©2017 www.challenginglearning.com

ACTIVITY:
What is a toy?
1-6
A doll

©2017 www.challenginglearning.com

ACTIVITY:
What is a toy?
1-7
A ball

©2017 www.challenginglearning.com

ACTIVITY:
What is a toy?
1-8
A dress

©2017 www.challenginglearning.com

ACTIVITY:
What is a toy?
1-9
Sea shells

©2017 www.challenginglearning.com

ACTIVITY:
What is a toy?
1-10
A tent

©2017 www.challenginglearning.com

ACTIVITY:
What is a toy?
1-11
A kitten

©2017 www.challenginglearning.com

ACTIVITY:
What is a toy?
1-12
A hamster

©2017 www.challenginglearning.com

ACTIVITY:
What is a toy?
1-13

A friend

©2017 www.challenginglearning.com

ACTIVITY:
What is a toy?
1-14

A story book

©2017 www.challenginglearning.com

ACTIVITY:
What is a toy?
1-15

Colouring pencils and book

©2017 www.challenginglearning.com

ACTIVITY:
What is a toy?
1-16

A pen and paper

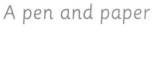

©2017 www.challenginglearning.com

ACTIVITY:
What is a toy?
1-17

Money

©2017 www.challenginglearning.com

ACTIVITY:
What is a toy?
1-18

A teddy bear

©2017 www.challenginglearning.com

ACTIVITY:
What is a toy?
1-19

A bike

©2017 www.challenginglearning.com

ACTIVITY:
What is a toy?
1-20

A car

©2017 www.challenginglearning.com

ACTIVITY:
What is a toy?
1-21

A mobile phone

©2017 www.challenginglearning.com

ACTIVITY:
What is a toy?
1-22

Food

©2017 www.challenginglearning.com

ACTIVITY:
What is a toy?
1-23

A torch

©2017 www.challenginglearning.com

ACTIVITY:
What is a toy?
1-24

Building bricks

©2017 www.challenginglearning.com

Activity 2:

People who help us

Young children are often told to ask for help from those around them, though they do not always consider what 'help' means or how to judge whom to ask in which context and why.

KEY CONCEPT

Help

KEY WORDS

Help, trust, care for, judge, reason, explain, job, best, worst, job, role, expert, helper

LEARNING INTENTION

To be able to judge whom to ask for help in different situations

SUCCESS CRITERIA

We can:

- Explain what we think help is and what help looks, sounds and feels like.
- Talk about people who have helped us in our daily life.
- Identify people who might be the 'experts' in certain jobs or roles.
- Compare different ways of helping people.
- Think about some of the dangers of asking for help (as well as the good points).

STRATEGY USED

Ranking

1. IDENTIFY IMPORTANT CONCEPTS

Some of the key areas to investigate within and around the concept of 'help' are the following:

- What 'help' looks like
- What trust means and how we know whom to trust when asking for help
- The different ways adults help
- The different ways other children might help
- Helping with feelings
- Help from experts
- Stranger danger
- Recognising when help is needed
- Personal relationships

2. CHALLENGE CHILDREN'S UNDERSTANDING

Figure 63 presents some examples of cognitive conflict we expect your children to experience.

Figure 63: Cognitive conflict about help

Opinion	Conflicting opinion
Help means doing something for someone else.	You can also help yourself.
Helping someone makes things easier for them.	Doing things that are harder to do helps you to get fit.
We should always help other people.	Sometimes people do not want or need help.
If I get lost, I am told to ask an adult for help.	I am told not to talk to strangers.
Someone helping me makes me feel good.	Too much help will make me lazy.

Create challenge using some of these questions:

- What does it mean to help someone?
- Is it always good to help others?
- Is it good to ask for help?
- Can help ever be a bad thing?
- Can you help someone too much?
- Should we try to help ourselves first before asking someone else to help us?
- Is there a difference between adults or strangers helping us and our friends giving us help?
- How do you know whether someone will be helpful or not?
- Do you need to trust someone in order for her to help you?
- Is everyone equally able to help us?

- What is the difference between someone helping us to do something and someone doing it for us?
- What makes some people better at helping than other people?
- Can you help someone by doing nothing?

3. CONSTRUCT UNDERSTANDING TOGETHER

Help your children make sense of their thoughts using one or more of the following activities:

1   Introduce the idea of the Ranking Frame shown in Figure 64, explaining that the best choice is at the top, the worst choice is at the bottom, with OK choices in the middle.

2   Share the people cards found in Figure 65 (page 142) with your children, and ask for their ideas about what the roles of the people are on each of the cards.

3   Go through the following range of scenarios one by one with your children. Each time, ask them to select a person by picking up a card or pointing to their chosen one and explaining why they have made that choice. Focus only on the best choice to begin with by placing that at the top of the Ranking Frame.

Who would be the best person to help if I wanted to:

- Build a wall
- Stop feeling unwell
- Make my cat better
- Get my hair cut
- Put out a fire
- Bake a cake

Now move to scenarios with less obvious answers:

- Find my way home
- Listen to a bedtime story
- Have fun
- Stop crying
- Feel good about myself
- Hear a funny story
- Be safe
- Learn something new

Figure 64: Ranking Frame with four options

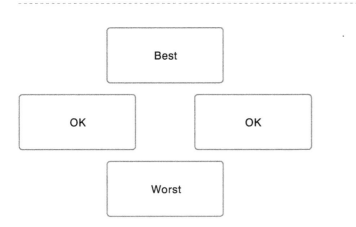

Once your children are confident in giving answers, begin using other parts of the Ranking Frame:

- Who would be the best to help us if there was a fire?

  They will most likely put the firefighter in the top spot, but whom would they choose to place in the two middle spots, and in the bottom spot?4

- Who would be the worst person for helping us if there was a fire?

  There will be a number of answers for this one, and each should be tested against reasoning and placed in the bottom spot.

- Which people would be 'just OK' for helping us if there was a fire?

  Again, there will be a variety of answers, which should be questioned and placed in the middle spots in the frame once your children have reached an agreement.

The following types of questions will deepen the dialogue:

- When would the builder be the best person to help us? For example, if we wanted to build a house.
- Is there any situation where the builder wouldn't be the best person to help us do this?
- What if it was a model house, a sandcastle or a computer game house, would he still be the best person?
- Who would be the worst person to help us do this? Why?
- Does anyone have a different answer? Why?
- Would that always be the case?
- Would it be the same person if you were at home or at school?

It is important that your children are expected to place a value on the cards, prioritise, make judgements and create a hierarchy. It is critical that they understand why they have done so.

- Are you saying that this person would be a better/worse help than that person? Why?
- In what ways would this person be a better/worse help that that person?
- Would anyone be exactly the same help as this person? Why?

Extension

To adapt the activity, you can reduce the number of people cards you are considering at any one time and do a simple best-and-worst rank.

To extend the activity, the Ranking Frame could be increased to a Diamond Nine format so that your children evaluate more cards in relation to one another at the same time.

4. CONSIDER THE LEARNING JOURNEY

The children can respond to the following review statements with:

Thumbs up – yes

Thumbs down – no

Thumbs to side – not sure

- I understand what it means to help someone.
- I understand how to decide/judge whom I should ask for help if I need it.
- We can be more help to someone if we know how to help.
- We are all able to help another person if he needs it.
- It is better to ask for help from someone we know well.

After each show of thumbs, the children can be given an opportunity to share their thoughts and reflections on the statement.

Transfer activities

Your children could become Help Detectives for a day and observe, investigate and record all the different forms of help they encounter. They can look for and think about some of the following information:

- Who is helping?
- Whom is being helped?
- What does the help look like?
- What does the help sound like?

Some stories and picture books to further explore the concept of 'help' are:

- *The Little Red Hen* (old folk tale).
- *The Elves and the Shoemaker* by the Brothers Grimm.
- *The Selfish Crocodile* by Faustin Charles.

Figure 65: Activity Cards: 'People who help us'

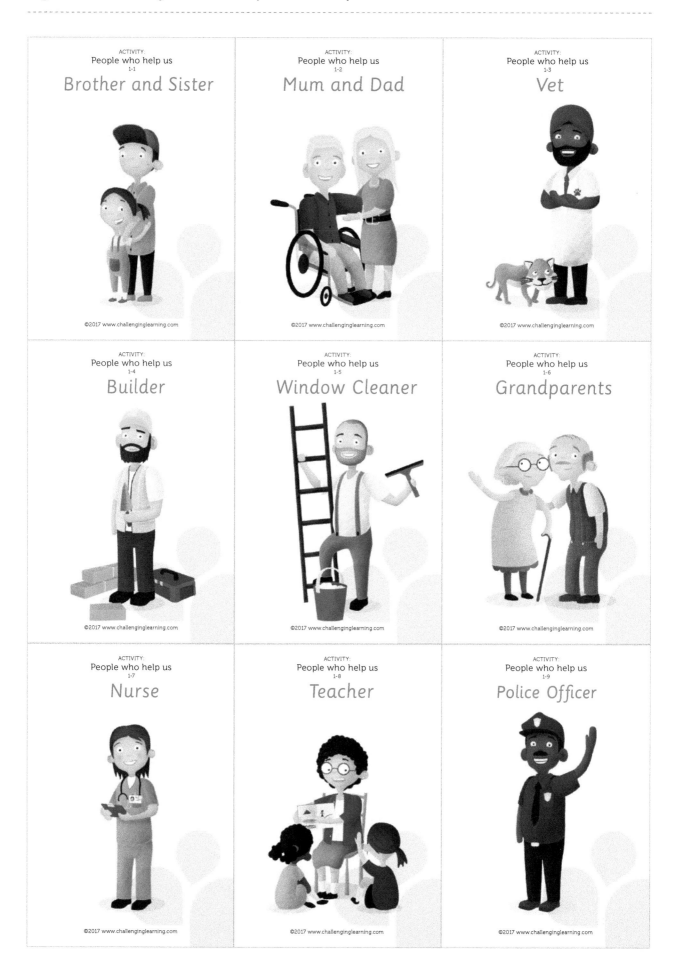

Hairdresser

Friends

Firefighters

Shop Assistant

Babysitter

Activity 3:

The Gingerbread Man

Making decisions and having choices are important aspects of early learning. Even a young baby makes a choice when she reaches out for one of the two objects in front of her. Encouraging all children to express and act on their preferences builds and strengthens a sense of responsibility for themselves and the notion that they are active contributors to their own and others' experiences.

KEY CONCEPT

Choice

KEY WORDS

Metal, wood, material, hard, soft, waterproof, not waterproof, large, small, light heavy, solid, has holes in it, will sink, will float

LEARNING INTENTION

To be able to think carefully about the choices we make

SUCCESS CRITERIA

We can:

- Talk about what a choice is.
- Think about the different choices we make each day.
- Recognise what we have to do to make a choice.
- Decide upon what would be a good choice and what would be a bad choice and say why.
- Use key words to explain our reasons for the choices we make.

STRATEGIES USED

Ranking

Opinion Line

1. IDENTIFY IMPORTANT CONCEPTS

Some of the key areas to investigate within and around the concept of 'choice' are the following:

- What 'choice' means
- Making my own choices
- Making choices together
- The responsibility of choice
- The right to choose
- Good choices and bad choices

Resources

Raincoat, bricks, water, rocks, wheelbarrow, toy fox, gingerbread men, toy boat, Wellington boots, buckets, basket, cardboard box, ball, spades, sticks, rubber duck, swimming costume, story book, cling film, rope, watering can.

Set up

Create a river bed using the raincoat, place some bricks under the raincoat to help create banks on either side. Use the wheelbarrow to hold water, which can be tipped, from one end of the 'river' to create flow, current and ripples. Place resources on the banks of river. Retell or re-enact the story.

'Run, run, as fast as you can, you can't catch me, I'm The Gingerbread Man!'

Ask the questions:

- Who is chasing The Gingerbread Man?
- Where can he go?

He needs to cross the river.

Ask the questions:

- How can he cross the river?
- What can he use?
- How deep is the river?
- How wide is the river?

Encourage your children to act out the various suggestions.

2. CHALLENGE CHILDREN'S UNDERSTANDING

Figure 66 presents some examples of cognitive conflict we expect your children to experience.

Create challenge using some of these questions:

- What is a choice?
- What choices do you make?
- What choices have you made today?
- What do we mean by a 'good' choice?
- What do we mean by a 'bad' choice?
- How do we know when we are making a good choice?
- What happens if we make a bad choice?

Figure 66: Cognitive conflict about choice

Opinion	Conflicting opinion
I always have a choice.	Some things I have to do because I am told to.
I don't want to choose whom to play with, so I will play with everyone.	By not choosing one person to play with, I have made a choice to play with everyone.
It is harder to make a choice when you only have two things to choose between.	It is harder to choose when you have lots of things to choose from.

- Is it good to have choices?

- What makes some choices difficult and some choices easy?

- Should you always make your own choices?

- When should other people choose for you?

- Is it impossible to not make any choice at all?

3. CONSTRUCT UNDERSTANDING TOGETHER

Help your children make sense of their thoughts using some of the following questions and activities.

Activity 1: Ranking

1   Introduce the Ranking Frame shown in Figure 64 (page 139), explaining that the best choice is at the top, the worst choice is at the bottom and OK choices are in the middle.

2   Allow your children the opportunity to investigate the resources in front of them. Handle them, talk about them, test them out and look at connections between any of the resources.

   Encourage your children to think about positive and negative qualities for the different choice options in relation to their properties: metal, wood, material, hard, soft, waterproof, not waterproof, large, small, light heavy, solid, has holes in it, will sink, will float, etc.

3   Ask your children to choose the best and worst ways of crossing the river for The Gingerbread Man. This can be done physically by moving the object cards into the ranking positions. Encourage your children to give reasons for each of their choices.

4   It is important that your children place a value on the cards and judge them in relation to one another. The following questions can help them do this:

   - Why do you think X would be the best choice?

   - Why do you think this would be better than Y or Z?

   - What makes X a good choice and Y a bad choice?

   - Why is Z only OK compared to X?

5   Provide your children with the opportunity re-rank or rearrange the order or priority of the choices to reflect any changes to their thinking.

ADAPTATION

Consider splitting the activity over two sessions, with an at-home session in between. Invite your children's families to think about some of these questions:

- How many choices do you make before breakfast?

- How many choices do others make for you each day?

- What is the most important choice you have had to make?

- Is there anything that you make the same choice about every day?

EXTENSION

To extend the challenge, you could go for any of these options:

1   Increase the number of cards to rank from a Diamond Four to a Diamond Nine.

2   Best Bag: Introduce a bag or a box filled with different descriptive word cards. The children choose an alternative for 'best' to help The Gingerbread Man decide the best way to cross the river. The words you provide could include:

    fastest, safest, quietest, most fun, easiest, scariest, wettest.

3   Weather Bag: introduce a bag containing weather words:

    sunshine, rain, snow, wind, ice, clouds.

    Let your children take turns in selecting a card and re-evaluating their ranking choices according to the different weather conditions.

    - What would be the best way for The Gingerbread Man to cross the river if it was raining?

    - What would be the best way for The Gingerbread Man to cross the river if it was icy?

    - What would be the best way for The Gingerbread Man to cross the river if it was sunny?

4   River Bag: Introduce a bag containing picture cards of different river conditions:

    wide, narrow, calm, fast, rocky, deep, shallow

    Let your children take turns in selecting a card and as a group re-evaluating their ranking choices according to the different weather conditions:

    - What would be the best way for The Gingerbread Man to cross a rocky river?

    - What would be the best way for The Gingerbread Man to cross a narrow river?

4. CONSIDER THE LEARNING JOURNEY

Provide your children with the opportunity to reflect on the learning process and talk about the following areas:

- What does it feel like to make a choice?

- How easy is it to make choices?

- Is it easier or harder to make a choice if there are lots of things to choose from?

- How important is it to make the 'right' choices?

Activity 2: Opinion Line

Use an Opinion Line to help your children clarify their thinking.

Use a rope to replicate the line shown in Figure 67. You could place a card with big, smiley face or thumbs up at the 'agree' end of the line and a sad face or thumbs down at the 'disagree' end

Figure 67: Opinion Line with smiley faces

AGREE   DISAGREE

of the line. Explain the meaning of these to your children, as well as what the line in between represents.

Use the following statements one at a time:

1   I am good at making choices.

2   It is good to have a choice.

3   We should always choose things by ourselves.

4   We should let other people choose for us.

5   It is easy to make a choice.

6   We should think carefully about every choice we make.

After each statement, ask your children to stand on the line. The more strongly they agree with the statement, the nearer the smiley face/thumbs up end of the line they should stand. The more they disagree, the nearer the sad face/thumbs down end of the line they should stand. If they really can't decide, they would stand exactly in the middle. They could also give reasons why they have chosen to stand where they have.

Transfer activity

Play the game *Good Choice, Bad Choice* by presenting your children with a number of choices to make, such as:

*   Eat your vegetables.

*   Cross the road without a grown-up.

*   Get wet in the rain.

*   Jump in muddy puddles.

*   Wear a sun hat in the summer.

*   Paint a picture using only red paint.

*   Follow the rules.

*   Feed your pet.

See Figure 68. Your children should use their thumbs up to show if they feel this is a good choice to make and thumbs down if they feel it is a bad choice and thumb to the side if they think it could be good and bad. Ask them for their reasons for their answers, and encourage other children to agree or disagree and share their own reasons why.

Resource cards for all these items are supplied with this lesson (see Figures 69–71), or you could use the physical objects.

Figure 68: Simple Ranking Frame with thumbs

GOOD

GOOD

BAD

GOOD

BAD

BAD

Figure 69: Activity Cards: 'The Gingerbread Man' – Set 1

ACTIVITY:
Gingerbread Man
1-1
Raincoat
©2017 www.challenginglearning.com

ACTIVITY:
Gingerbread Man
1-2
Bricks
©2017 www.challenginglearning.com

ACTIVITY:
Gingerbread Man
1-3
Water
©2017 www.challenginglearning.com

ACTIVITY:
Gingerbread Man
1-4
Rocks
©2017 www.challenginglearning.com

ACTIVITY:
Gingerbread Man
1-5
Wheel Barrow
©2017 www.challenginglearning.com

ACTIVITY:
Gingerbread Man
1-6
Fox
©2017 www.challenginglearning.com

ACTIVITY:
Gingerbread Man
1-7
Gingerbread Man
©2017 www.challenginglearning.com

ACTIVITY:
Gingerbread Man
1-8
Boat
©2017 www.challenginglearning.com

ACTIVITY:
Gingerbread Man
1-9
Wellington Boots
©2017 www.challenginglearning.com

ACTIVITY:
Gingerbread Man
1-19
Clingfilm

ACTIVITY:
Gingerbread Man
1-20
Rope

ACTIVITY:
Gingerbread Man
1-21
Watering Can

ACTIVITY:
Gingerbread Man
1-22
Fins

Figure 70: Activity Cards: 'The Gingerbread Man" – Set 2

ChallengingLEARNING | 8. Early learning activities Activity 3: The Gingerbread Man

Figure 71: Activity Cards: 'The Gingerbread Man' – Set 3

ACTIVITY:
Gingerbread Man
3-1

Wide River

©2017 www.challenginglearning.com

ACTIVITY:
Gingerbread Man
3-2

Narrow River

©2017 www.challenginglearning.com

ACTIVITY:
Gingerbread Man
3-3

Deep River

©2017 www.challenginglearning.com

ACTIVITY:
Gingerbread Man
3-4

Shallow River

©2017 www.challenginglearning.com

ACTIVITY:
Gingerbread Man
3-5

Rocky River

©2017 www.challenginglearning.com

ACTIVITY:
Gingerbread Man
3-6

Calm River

©2017 www.challenginglearning.com

ACTIVITY:
Gingerbread Man
3-7

Fast River

©2017 www.challenginglearning.com

Activity 4:

Why is Teddy feeling unwell?

Young children often confuse the term 'unwell' with any kind of hurt (physical or emotional) or with negative feelings. Developing the language and reasoning for describing more accurately their feelings of being unwell is an important aspect of early learning, which is why we have created this 'Mystery'.

KEY CONCEPT

Illness (being unwell)

KEY WORDS

Unwell, ill, fear, worry, tiredness, grumpiness, greed, safety, activity, sport, healthy, unhealthy, upset, sad, sick, symptom

LEARNING INTENTION

To understand what it means to be unwell

SUCCESS CRITERIA

We can:

- Talk about our own experiences of being unwell.
- Compare different feelings and symptoms of being unwell.
- Identify things that could make us and Teddy feel unwell.
- Sort information to make sense of it.
- Work together to solve a problem and reach a group decision.

STRATEGY USED

Mystery

1. IDENTIFY IMPORTANT CONCEPTS

Sit in a circle with your children, and explain that you have a Mystery to solve. Introduce everybody to a Teddy bear or soft toy and say, 'Teddy has been feeling very unwell today, and I was hoping you would help me discover why'.

Ask your children to think about their own experiences of being unwell and what they did. It is good to unpack these ideas and test them against general and specific examples, each time returning to the key questions:

- What does it mean to be 'unwell'?
- Would X make Teddy unwell?
- Is X the same as being unwell?

2. CHALLENGE CHILDREN'S UNDERSTANDING

Figure 72 presents some examples of cognitive conflict we expect your children to experience.

Figure 72: Cognitive conflict about being unwell

Opinion	Conflicting opinion
When I am unwell, I feel really bad.	I feel really bad when I get into trouble, but I am not unwell.
If you have tummy ache, you are unwell.	I get tummy ache when I am really excited about something.
Being unwell is always horrible.	When I am unwell, I get extra cuddles and attention, which is nice.

Create challenge using some of these questions:

- What does 'unwell' mean?
- How do you feel when you are 'unwell'?
- Can you feel unwell but still be well?
- What is the difference between being sad and being unwell?
- What is the difference between being hurt and being unwell?
- What is the difference between being tired and being unwell?
- What is the difference between being worried and being unwell?
- Can you be unwell without being sad?
- Is there anything good about being unwell?
- Do we always need medicine to make us well again?
- What things help you to feel well again if you have been ill?
- Why do you think some things make us feel unwell and some don't?
- Do we all feel the same way when we are unwell?
- Is being unwell different for adults and children?
- What do you think being unwell is like for animals?

3. CONSTRUCT UNDERSTANDING

Help your children make sense of their thoughts using one or more of the following activities.

With your children still sat in the circle, return the discussion to Teddy, saying:

> Teddy is still feeling unwell, and we need to find out what is wrong with him. Can you help me look at the clues and try and work it out?

Introduce the Mystery cards (Figure 73) and read them out one at a time. Draw attention to the picture and place them all face up in the centre of the circle.

Ask your children to identify any clues that they think might be important; for example, one child might pick up the picture of three bananas and say, 'I think Teddy is unwell because he ate all the bananas, and it gave him a tummy ache'.

Encourage your children to justify their decisions with reasons, using some of the following questions to encourage them further:

- Why do you think that made him unwell?

- Is that the only reason he is unwell?

- Is that the most important reason for him being unwell?

- Does everyone agree?

- Does anyone disagree and think this did not make him unwell?

- Does anyone think that there is a different reason for him being unwell that is more important than this one?

- Are there any clues that you feel are definitely *not* reasons for his being unwell?

You can support your children to sort the information cards in some of these different ways:

- Good clues, bad clues, not sure

- Make links between cards with common information

- Physically unwell and emotionally unwell

Help your children to talk about the sorting criteria they use as they place the clues into groups. For example, if they decide unwell means having a tummy ache, then cards relating to this should go into one pile and other clues into another pile.

Alternatively, they can place the clues on a line of rope or string with the most significant clue at one end and the least significant at the other end. They should evaluate each piece of information in relation to the rest of the clues.

EXTENSION

To extend the activity, you could ask your children to consider what information is missing and to separate clues that say what *did* happen from clues that say what *might* have happened.

For example, we are told:

- Teddy went to a party.

- He played lots of football.

- He ate two small cakes and three bananas and some berries from a bush.

- He drank lots of orange juice.

- He got up very early.

- He liked to have a lie-in.

We are not told:

- What else he ate that day.

- What else he ate at the party.

- If the berries were safe to eat or not, at what time he ate these things.

- If he ate them all at once.

- If he had any allergies or intolerances.

- If he was feeling unwell before he went to the party.

- If he was feeling unwell before he ate or drank any of the things listed.

- What kind of party he went to

- When he played football.

- If he likes parties or football.

NB: Encourage your children to question the relevance of the missing information.

We can guess:

- He got a tummy ache from eating all the food at once.

- The berries from the bush were inedible, so they made him unwell.

- He ate the food and drank the juice, then jumped around at the party and played football with a full tummy, which made him feel unwell.

- He was very hungry as he had only snacked on things over the course of the day, and this made him have a tummy ache.

- The party was a football party.

- The party was in the morning, and he played football all afternoon, and this made him tired, which gave him a headache.

- He had a tummy bug, caught from another child at the party, and this made him unwell.

- He had a tummy bug or a head cold, and it had nothing to do with any of the clue cards.

- He got hit on the head with the football, and this made him feel unwell.

4. CONSIDER THE LEARNING JOURNEY

Your children should consider how they came to their decision and the process they went through to get there. These questions should help to prompt their thinking:

- How did you decide on what made Teddy unwell?

- Is it important to agree on an answer together?

- Which clues really helped?

- If there had been no clue cards, how could you have solved the Mystery?

Transfer activities

- Encourage your children to find out from their parents which childhood illnesses they have already had and what the symptoms and treatments for those were and how long the illness lasted.

- You could move your children's attention on to how to prevent illness and the concept of 'being healthy'. They can look at healthy eating, exercise, good personal hygiene, simple food hygiene and immunisation.

- Encourage your children to set up a Teddy bear treatment centre where they help all poorly teddies to get better.

Figure 73: Activity Cards: 'Why is Teddy feeling unwell?'

Teddy was at a party

Teddy was playing games late at night

Teddy went out in the rain

Activity 5:

Decisions, decisions

Making decisions and having choices are so important to childhood development that we have created a second resource to help you develop your children's decision-making abilities (the first resource is shown in Activity 3). Young children often have many, if not most decisions made for them. This activity is aimed at helping them to understand what decisions are and how to make them. This can help with confidence and understanding cause and effect.

KEY CONCEPT

Making decisions

KEY WORDS

Decisions, choices, challenge, reason, information, comparing, like, dislike, interesting

LEARNING INTENTION

To be able to give reasons for the decisions we make

SUCCESS CRITERIA

We can:

- Understand what it means to make a decision.
- Recognise when we make decisions.
- Consider the good and bad points of something before making a decision about it.
- Prioritise our options so that we can make good decisions.
- Think about the consequences of our decisions.

STRATEGY USED

Diamond Ranking

1. IDENTIFY IMPORTANT CONCEPTS

Some of the key areas to investigate within and around the concept of 'making decisions' are:

- The role of decision making in everyday life.

- The way in which decisions are made.

- The consequences of making successful or unsuccessful decisions.

- The element of 'choice' involved in decision making.

- Identifying different options in the decision-making process.

- Exploring alternative viewpoints when making decisions.

2. CHALLENGE CHILDREN'S UNDERSTANDING

Figure 74 presents some examples of cognitive conflict we expect your children to experience.

Figure 74: Cognitive conflict about making decisions

Opinion	Conflicting opinion
It is good to make our own decisions.	Adults know best and should make decisions for us.
We should not make bad decisions.	We learn a lot from bad decisions.
It is really hard to make decisions.	Deciding what to choose for my snack is easy.

Create challenge using some of these questions:

- What is a decision?

- What have you done today?

- When did you have to make a decision today?

- What did you decide to do?

- What did you *have* to do?

- How do you make a decision?

- Is it easy to decide on something?

- Who can help you to decide on something?

- How can they help?

- How do you know you have made a good decision?

- How can you get better at making decisions?

- Is making a decision the same as choosing?

- How many decisions were involved in the following?

    - I got out of bed.

    - I got out of bed because my mum told me to.

    - I got out of bed because I had to get dressed.

    - I cried out in pain when someone bumped into me in the park, and my mum took me home.

3. CONSTRUCT UNDERSTANDING TOGETHER

Help your children make sense of their thoughts using some of these questions and activities.

Explain to your children that a wizard has been to visit and has left a selection of gifts for the group, but they can only keep one of them. They must make the decision together about which gift to keep.

Introduce your children to the activity cards (Figure 75) showing all the different possible gifts on offer.

- Your children should explore the gifts in front of them and identify what they are.

- They can begin to sort the presents using their own criteria. This may include:

    What they like most.

    What they dislike most.

    The most interesting.

    The most useful.

    The most needed.

    The ones they have most questions about.

- Encourage them to compare gifts and make links:

    Why is that one more interesting than this one?

    Why do you think these two are as useful as one another?

    Are you saying that you like this gift better than any other gift?

    What makes this one less needed than these two?

Discuss with your children that one way to help them to make a decision is to sort all the options they have into which are most important to them and the least important to them. Explain that this is called 'prioritising' and is an important skill in helping us to make decisions.

- Introduce your children to the simple Ranking Frame shown in Figure 64 (page 139), and demonstrate how they can place the gifts on the frame depending on how important they feel they are to them. They should use their judgements of the gifts to help them to make a decision about which one to keep.

- They should place the most important one to keep at the top of the frame, the least important at the bottom and decide on two that they feel are of average importance to place in the middle.

- Alternatively, they can narrow their decision down to their four favourite gifts and rank them first, joint second and third.

You can question the assumptions being made by your children throughout the dialogue. Encourage them to consider alternate viewpoints, to decide between different options and to deepen their thinking with additional questions:

If they choose the flying carpet:

    How do they know it will go where they want it to?

    What can they do to make sure they get home again?

    What happens if they want to come home early?

    How do you know it is safe?

    What if there are no ways of controlling it?

    What if it doesn't like passengers?

    How important would it be to have a flying carpet in their life?

If they choose the magic box:

How do they know if the box is big enough?

How will they choose what is inside the box?

What if they have no choice about what is in the box?

What happens if they don't like what is in the box?

Is it good magic or bad magic?

How long does the magic last?

What if the box is empty because it makes things disappear?

What do we mean by magic?

How important would it be to have a magic box in their life?

If they choose the magic chocolate box:

What magic would it be able to do?

How will they choose what types of chocolate to have?

What happens if it keeps on filling up?

What happens to the chocolates if they don't eat them?

If the chocolates are magic, will they taste different? Good or bad?

Are they safe to eat?

Will the chocolates do magical things too?

How do they know it really is magical?

How important would it be to have a magic chocolate box in their life?

If they choose the singing frogs:

How will they choose the songs that are sung?

How will they stop the frogs from singing?

What happens if they can't turn the volume up and down?

How do they know that the frogs are good singers?

What happens to the frogs if they stop singing?

Do the frogs need special care and food and lots of attention?

Are they friendly?

How important would it be to have singing frogs in their life?

If they choose a magic fruit tree:

What magic would it be able to do?

How will they choose the types of fruit it grows?

Is it better if it keeps on growing or stays the same size? Why?

Where will they put it?

Do they know how to look after it?

How do they know it will always produce fruit?

How important would it be to have a fruit tree in their life?

If they choose a rainbow:

What will they do with it?

What will they find at the end of it?

Does it matter if it can be seen by other people? Why?

What if it disappears once the sun goes in?

What if it always brings rain with it?

What if it always brings the sun with it?

Where would you keep it?

How long would it last?

How important would it be to have a rainbow in their life?

If they choose an elephant:

Where would they keep it?

What will they do with it?

How will they make sure it isn't lonely?

What are the dangers of owning an elephant?

What if it didn't like people?

How much food and care would it need?

How important would it be to have an elephant in their life?

If they choose a magic telephone:

What magic would it be able to do?

What happens if it phones the wrong person?

Does it have any special powers?

Can they choose whom to phone?

Can they choose who calls them?

How important would it be to have a magic telephone in their life?

If they choose an invisibility hat:

What happens if they become visible too soon?

Why would it be useful to be invisible?

When is it a bad idea to be invisible?

What if they can't become visible again?

Is the hat still visible if they are invisible?

How many times can it be used before it runs out?

Does it work on objects and animals or only on people?

How important would it be to have an invisibility hat in their life?

ADAPTATION

You can use objects in the place of the resource cards with younger children and reduce the number of objects or cards being considered at any one time.

EXTENSION

Added challenge can be introduced in the level of questioning and language used that will impact on the depth of the inquiry. You can also challenge your children more by using a Diamond Nine Ranking Frame and to prioritise nine gifts in relation to one another.

4. REVIEWING THE LEARNING JOURNEY

At the end of the activity, it is usual to encourage your children to review their learning journey and the thinking progress they have engaged in throughout the session.

This can include reflection on the thinking that has taken place to this point and a summary and conclusion of the new understanding reached.

Thoughtful reflection

Encourage your children to consider the thinking skills that they have used during this activity in order to make a decision:

- What skills have they used?

- When did they use them?

- How successfully did they use them?

- How do they know?

- Which skills could they use next time?

Summary

Allow your children the opportunity to reflect on the way in which they have ranked the cards and decisions they have made throughout the activity.

If they have worked in separate small groups, then they can share their Ranking Frame with the other groups and explain their decisions and the reasons behind them.

If they have worked as one whole group, they should think about all the decisions they made during the activity and what skills they used to reach a collective decision.

All of your children should reflect on the following questions:

- Why is it important to make good decisions?

- What do we need to think about when making a decision?

- How do we know we've made a good decision?

- How can we become better decision makers?

- How can we help one another to make decisions?

Transfer activities

- Your children could keep a 'decision diary' at home for the week. They can record the different decisions they make and code them red, yellow or green depending on whether they were difficult, OK or easy decisions to make.

- Provide opportunities for your children to make decisions for themselves and the group throughout the week, and create reflection time to discuss and think about the types of decisions they made, the consequences of the decisions, the importance of them and how it made them feel. They could decide on:

    The book for story time.

    The choice of afternoon activities available.

    Whom to sit next to for lunch.

    Whom to partner with for certain activities.

    Which clothes to dress up in during role play.

    What colour paints to use for their artwork.

    How many people should be allowed in the role-play area at one time.

    When story time should be.

Figure 75: Activity Cards: 'Decisions, decisions'

ACTIVITY:
Decisions, Decisions
1-1

A magic box!

©2017 www.challenginglearning.com

ACTIVITY:
Decisions, Decisions
1-2

A flying carpet!

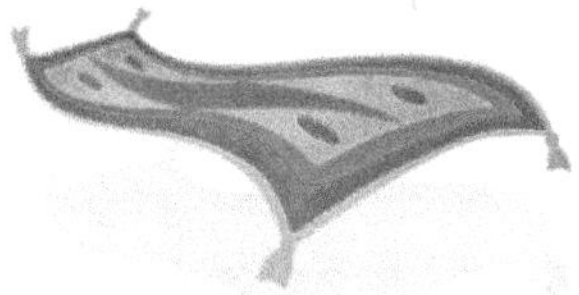

©2017 www.challenginglearning.com

ACTIVITY:
Decisions, Decisions
1-3

A magic chocolate box!

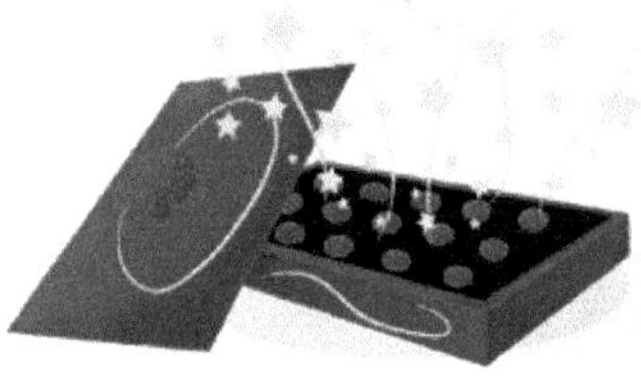

©2017 www.challenginglearning.com

ACTIVITY:
Decisions, Decisions
1-4

Singing frogs!

©2017 www.challenginglearning.com

ACTIVITY:
Decisions, Decisions
1-5

A rainbow!

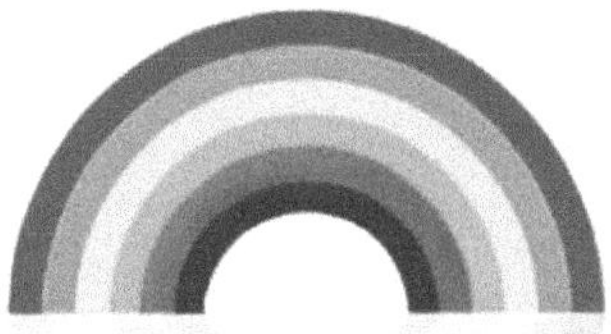

©2017 www.challenginglearning.com

ACTIVITY:
Decisions, Decisions
1-6

An elephant!

©2017 www.challenginglearning.com

ACTIVITY:
Decisions, Decisions
1-7

An invisibility hat!

©2017 www.challenginglearning.com

ACTIVITY:
Decisions, Decisions
1-8

A fruit tree!

©2017 www.challenginglearning.com

ACTIVITY:
Decisions, Decisions
1-9

A magic phone!

©2017 www.challenginglearning.com

Activity 6:

Shape

Young children enjoy talking about and making shapes. Not only are shapes mathematical concepts, children can be imaginative and philosophical when thinking about questions such as, 'Does everything have a shape?' and 'What is the difference between the shape of a cloud and the shape of a triangle?'

KEY CONCEPTS

Shape and space

KEY WORDS

Red, yellow, blue, green

Big, small, medium, little, large

Above, below, next to, beside, under, in between

Square, circle, triangle, rectangle

LEARNING INTENTION

To be able to use accurate language to name common two-dimensional shapes and their colour and position

SUCCESS CRITERIA

We can:

- Talk about what a shape is and spot shapes around us.
- Match the names to the shapes of a circle, square, triangle and rectangle.
- Recognise the colour of the shapes.
- Describe the size of the shape by comparing it to other shapes.
- Use key words to explain the position of the shape.

STRATEGIES USED

Collaborative Memory

Ranking

1. IDENTIFY IMPORTANT CONCEPTS

Some of the key areas to investigate within and around the concepts of 'shape and space' are:

- The properties of regular two-dimensional shapes (size, number of sides, number of corners).
- Our understanding of shape within a space.
- How shapes are used around us.
- Relationships between, shape, size and position.

2. CHALLENGE CHILDREN'S UNDERSTANDING

Figure 76 presents some examples of cognitive conflict we expect your children to experience.

Figure 76: Cognitive conflict about shape

Opinion	Conflicting opinion
Shape is about how something looks.	Shape is about how something feels.
You can recognise things by their shape.	The shape of something can change, but its identity (what it is) can stay the same.
The world is full of shapes.	Some things seem to be shapeless.
Shapes have names.	There is no name for the shape of a butterfly's wing or for each different shape of clouds or leaves.

Create challenge using some of these questions:

- What is shape?
- What shapes can you see around you?
- How do you know something has a shape?
- Can you think of things that are always the same shape?
- Does everything have a shape?
- How can something be shapeless?
- If you change the shape of something, does it change what it is?
- If you changed shape, would you not be 'you' anymore?
- Why do we have shapes?
- Why is shape important?
- Does a shape change if we change its position? (For example, put it above our heads or turn it upside down?)
- What do you think about first when you see something: its size or its shape?
- What shape is the best?
- Which shape is most useful?

3. CONSTRUCT UNDERSTANDING TOGETHER

Help your children make sense of their thoughts using some of these questions and activities.

Hold each shape up in turn, beginning with a circle and ask the following questions:

- What is this shape called?
- How do we know this is a circle and not a square?
- What is the same about all circles? (Ask the same question of other shapes.)
- What is the different about this circle compared to this circle? (Hold two different coloured or sized circles up to be compared, and repeat with other shapes/sizes/colours.)

Place the circle next to the square and on top of the triangle, and ask the children to describe where the circle is, encouraging them to use positional vocabulary as well as size, shape and colour vocabulary.

- What is it next to/on top of/underneath/opposite/above/below/top/bottom/right of/left of?

Activity 1: Collaborative Memory

Use a baseboard and a selection of shapes of different sizes and colours to create a memory board. Figure 77 shows an example memory board.

The baseboard can be anything you like. If you partition the board into different coloured halves, quarters or eighths, it provides a structure for your children to identify and describe the position of the shapes more easily.

Do *not* show your children this yet.

The Memory Board you create for your children could be much simpler than the one in Figure 77 and have only three or four shapes on it to begin with or could be more challenging with more shapes and some shapes overlapping others. This will depend upon your children's existing knowledge and understanding of shape as well as their language development.

Figure 77: Memory Board

Organise your children into groups of three children, and give each group a baseboard and a set of the relevant shapes they need to complete their map.

- Number the children one, two and three, and ask all the number ones to be a 'spy'.

- Behind a screen, show them the memory map you have created.

- After a short time (15–30 seconds depending on the age and ability of the child), send them back to their group to describe where the shapes need to be positioned on the board.

- The spies are not allowed to touch the shapes or the board while they are still spies.

- Explain to your children that it is the job of the spy to look, remember and whisper information back to the group. The rest of the group have the job of listening carefully and following instructions.

- Once the groups have had one or two minutes to work on the information the spy has told them, the number two children become the spies, and the process gets repeated until all children have had a turn at being a spy.

At this stage, your children need to consider the accuracy of their memory map and how well they think they have done so far:

- How happy are you with the way your map looks?

- How much does your map look like the one behind the screen?

- What do you think you got right?

- Which parts do you think may be wrong?

- Which bit would you like to look at again?

- What could you do to try and remember more next time?

- Who remembered the most?

Give each child another turn at being a spy. Once everyone has had two turns, they should create their final map. The original design should now be revealed, and the groups should compare their own design to this and think about how well they did with the task.

- How well did each team member work as a spy?

- How well did each team member work as a listener?

- How well did you follow instructions?

- How well did you work as a team?

- How much do you know about shape and colour names now?

ADAPTATION

- Use fewer shapes.

- Create a simpler design.

- Give the children longer to spy and longer to feed back to the group.

- Give each child more turns to spy.

- Give them the exact shapes needed.

EXTENSION

- Use more shapes.

- Create a more complex design.

- Use additional 2D shapes.

- Introduce some 3D shapes.

- Give less spy time and feedback time.

- Give out more shapes than are needed so that your children have to sort out the relevant parts from the irrelevant.

4. CONSIDER THE LEARNING JOURNEY

Provide your children with the opportunity to reflect on the learning process and talk about the following areas:

- How close is their map to the original?
- How well did their group work as a team?
- What skills were used during the process?

Comparing their design to the original:

- Which parts are exactly the same?
- Which parts are almost the same?
- Which parts are very different?
- What would have made it easier to get it exactly the same?
- Is it possible to get it exactly the same?
- Why are some parts the same and some not?
- What made some parts easier or harder than others to copy?
- Which were the most difficult to remember? Why was this?
- Which parts were easiest to remember?

The quality of the group work:

- What things did your group do that worked really well?
- What things did not work quite so well?
- What would you do differently if you did the activity again?
- What would you do the same?
- Which role in the group did you like better, spy or listener?
- What was the most important role?

The knowledge and skills used and developed during the activity:

- Which shapes did you find the easiest to remember?
- Did knowing the size and colour of the shapes help you?
- Was it more difficult to describe the position, the size or the colour of the shape?
- What words or names did you find hardest to remember or use?
- What is the most important thing you need to know or do to do well in this activity?

Activity 2: Ranking

Share the skills cards shown in Figure 78 with your children. Talk about the skills on each of the cards and encourage them to think about how well they used these skills in their groups during the activity. Then show them the simple Ranking Frame in Figure 64 (page 139) and ask them to decide which of the skills cards should go at the top, which ones in the middle and which ones at the bottom.

Ask questions such as:

- Why do you think that skill is more important than this one?
- Does anyone disagree?
- Does anyone think there is a more important skill? Which one? Why?
- Are there any skills we did not need at all?
- What do we mean by important?

Transfer activities

- Hide some 2D and 3D shapes in a bag. Ask your children to dip their hand into the bag and choose a shape; without pulling it out, ask the children to describe the shape to the rest of the group according to its properties. If this is too challenging for the children, alternatively you could do it and describe the shape to the children.

- Create shape pictures using a range of 2D shapes.

- You could give children the outline of various 2D shapes and ask them to trace them by bending pipe cleaners.

- Show the children images of Kandinsky paintings, have the children identify as many shapes as they can find in the paintings and create a tally chart of how many times each shape was used by writing tally marks on the shapes.

- Take the children on a 'shape walk' to find shapes in and around the house/classroom/school. On the walk, you could take pictures of the children with shapes that they find, then put the pictures in a photo album

Figure 78: Activity Cards: 'Shape'

Remembering lots

Working together

Encouraging each other

Thinking carefully

Activity 7:

Fairy tales

If you want your children to be intelligent, read them fairy tales. If you want them to be more intelligent, read them more fairy tales. (Albert Einstein, quoted in Frayling, 2005)

KEY CONCEPT

Stories (fairy tales)

KEY WORDS

Fairy tale, story, character, good, bad, evil, magic, wolf, pig, bear

Same, different, in common, similar, sometimes, always, never

LEARNING INTENTION

To understand what makes a story a fairy tale

SUCCESS CRITERIA

We can:

- Listen to the stories of at least three fairy tales.
- Retell some of the important points of these stories.
- Identify who the characters are and what their roles are in the tale.
- Talk about important features of fairy tales.
- Compare two or three fairy tales and sort out what parts of the stories are the same and different.

STRATEGY USED

Venn Diagram

Ranking

1. IDENTIFY IMPORTANT CONCEPTS

Some of the key areas to investigate within and around the concept of 'fairy tales' are:

- Good/bad characters
- Magic
- Special beginning and ending words
- Special numbers
- Talking animals

2. CHALLENGE CHILDREN'S UNDERSTANDING

Figure 79 presents some examples of conflict we expect your children to experience.

Figure 79: Cognitive conflict about fairy tales

Opinion	Conflicting opinion
Fairy tales teach us the difference between right and wrong.	Many fairy tales involve someone being killed by another character.
Fairy tales have a 'good' character and a 'bad' character: *Red Riding Hood and the Wolf.*	The 'good' character is not always 'good': *Red Riding Hood disobeys her mother, breaks her promise, talks to strangers.*
Fairy tales have talking animals in them.	Many cartoons and stories have talking animals but are not fairy tales.

Create challenge using some of these questions:

- What is a fairy tale?
- Why do you think fairy tales are written?
- What would our lives be like without stories?
- Why do lots of stories have magic in them?
- What is your favourite fairy tale?
- What makes a story a 'good story'?
- Can animals really talk?
- What makes someone 'good' or 'bad'?
- Should all stories have a 'happy' ending?
- Why are some characters forgiven and others not?
- Are animals or people more important in fairy tales?
- Do fairy tales always have magic in them?
- Can a true story ever be a fairy tale?

3. CONSTRUCT UNDERSTANDING

Share the stories of *Little Red Riding Hood*, *Goldilocks and the Three Bears* and *The Three Little Pigs* with your children. This can be done over a series of sessions. Ensure that the children have a good understanding of the story, the plot and the characters involved.

Activity 1: Sorting and Classifying using a Venn Diagram

- Explain that all the different parts of the stories have been muddled up, and you need your children's help to sort them out.

- Introduce a red hoop, and explain to your children that anything to do with the story of *Little Red Riding Hood* should be placed in the red hoop. (See Figure 80.)

- Starting off with the more concrete cards (e.g. pig, wolf, house, girl), ask the children to consider the story and decide whether that card should go in the red hoop or not. Repeat this process with other cards, moving on to more abstract cards such as love, excited, nasty. Each time, ask your children to provide reasons to support their answers, and encourage them to refer to the story while doing so.

- Introduce a yellow hoop for Goldilocks and then a blue hoop for the Three Little Pigs and repeat the process each time.

- Ask your children to consider where they may place cards that would fit in more than one hoop, and demonstrate that the hoops can overlap to accommodate 'shared' cards.

- Demonstrate this first with two hoops, then with three if they have understood the idea well enough.

- Your children should now sort the cards between the three hoops, comparing and contrasting the stories to decide which 'cards' go into which space.

Figure 80: Venn Diagram of fairy tales

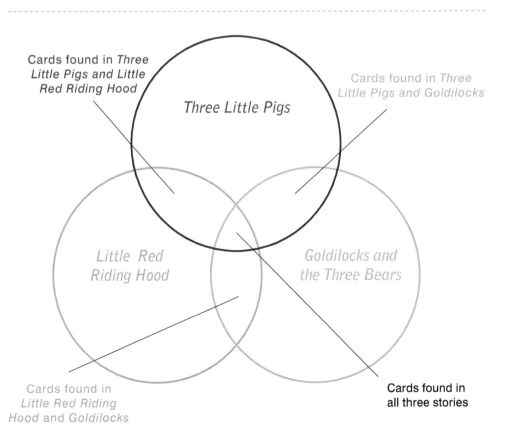

Cards found in *Three Little Pigs and Little Red Riding Hood*

Cards found in *Three Little Pigs and Goldilocks*

Three Little Pigs

Little Red Riding Hood

Goldilocks and the Three Bears

Cards found in *Little Red Riding Hood and Goldilocks*

Cards found in all three stories

ADAPTATION

To adapt the activity, consider only two stories at a time, and concentrate on the more concrete characteristic cards.

To extend the activity, compare two or three different versions of each story using the same Venn Diagram set-up and cards.

4. CONSIDER THE LEARNING JOURNEY

Ask your children to reflect on what they now know about fairy tales.

- What do all the fairy tales we looked at have in common?

- Why do you think we enjoy reading or hearing fairy tales?

Activity 2: Ranking

- A useful way for your children to sort through all their ideas is through Ranking.

- Ask your children to think about what they feel are the most important things in a fairy tale and which are the least important.

- Introduce the Ranking Frame shown in Figure 64 (page 139) and make use of the cards in Figure 81. Explain to your children that they must put the most important thing a fairy tale needs at the top of the frame in the smiley face box and the least important thing in the bottom box with the sad face. They should put things that are only fairly important in the middle boxes.

Encourage your children to give reasons for their choices and to compare the importance of each card against the others.

Transfer activities

- Invite your children to record themselves telling a fairy tale and listen to it.

- Children could join in drama hot-seating activities with one child taking on the role of a fairy tale character and the rest of the children asking her questions relating to the story. For example, asking Baby Bear how he felt when he discovered his chair had been broken.

Figure 81: Activity Cards: 'Fairy Tales'

ACTIVITY: Fairy Tales 1-1 **Pig** ©2017 www.challenginglearning.com	ACTIVITY: Fairy Tales 1-2 **Wolf** ©2017 www.challenginglearning.com	ACTIVITY: Fairy Tales 1-3 **Axe** ©2017 www.challenginglearning.com
ACTIVITY: Fairy Tales 1-4 **Girl** ©2017 www.challenginglearning.com	ACTIVITY: Fairy Tales 1-5 **Dad** ©2017 www.challenginglearning.com	ACTIVITY: Fairy Tales 1-6 **Scared** ©2017 www.challenginglearning.com
ACTIVITY: Fairy Tales 1-7 **Nasty** ©2017 www.challenginglearning.com	ACTIVITY: Fairy Tales 1-8 **Angry** ©2017 www.challenginglearning.com	ACTIVITY: Fairy Tales 1-9 **Bed** ©2017 www.challenginglearning.com

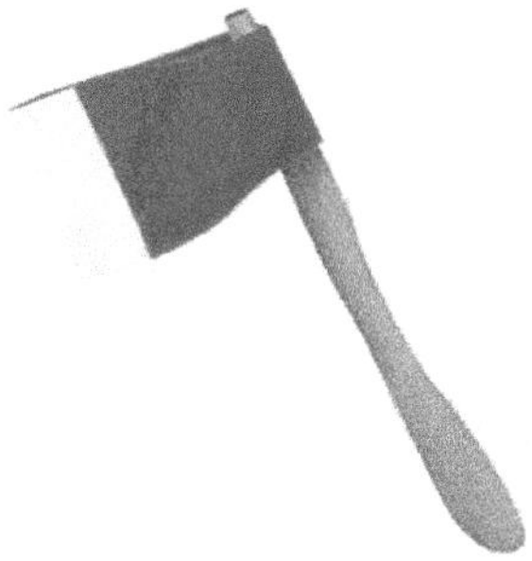

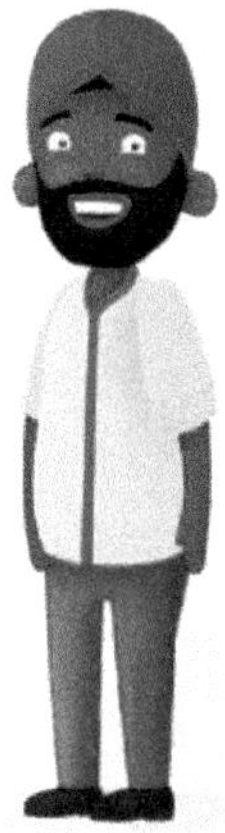

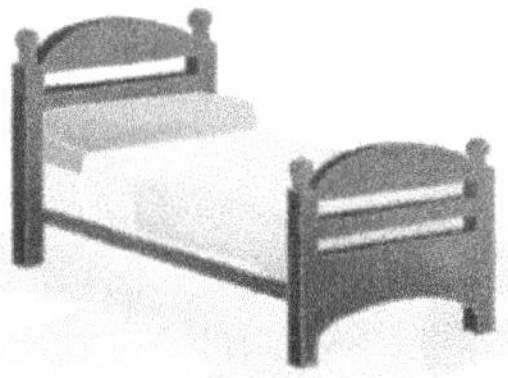

ACTIVITY:
Fairy Tales
1-10

House

ACTIVITY:
Fairy Tales
1-11

Happy

ACTIVITY:
Fairy Tales
1-12

Bear

ACTIVITY:
Fairy Tales
1-13

Three

ACTIVITY:
Fairy Tales
1-14

Sad

ACTIVITY:
Fairy Tales
1-15

Straw

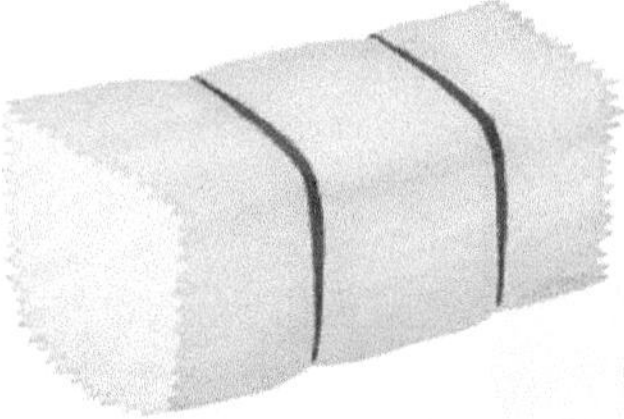

ACTIVITY:
Fairy Tales
1-16

Bricks

ACTIVITY:
Fairy Tales
1-17

Granny

ACTIVITY:
Fairy Tales
1-18

Mum

Activity 8:

Being a good friend

KEY CONCEPT

Friendship

KEY WORDS

Friends, friendship, friendliness, love, care, respect, honesty, thoughtfulness, listening, saying sorry, forgiving

LEARNING INTENTION

To understand what it means to be a friend

SUCCESS CRITERIA

We can:

- Describe what makes someone a friend.
- Say what friends should do.
- Say what friends should *not* do.
- Imagine a 'perfect friend'.
- Identify the most important things about friendship.

STRATEGY USED

Diamond Ranking

1. IDENTIFY IMPORTANT CONCEPTS

Some of the key ideas to investigate within and around the concept of 'friendship' are:

- The nature and meaning of friendship.
- How mutual caring relates to friendship.
- The importance of shared activity and interests.
- The value of friendship individually.
- The value of friendship socially.

2. CHALLENGE CHILDREN'S UNDERSTANDING

Figure 82 presents some examples of cognitive conflict we expect your children to experience.

Figure 82: Cognitive conflict about friends

Opinion	Conflicting opinion
A friend should share everything with you.	I don't want my friends to share their germs and illnesses with me.
Friends are nice to each other.	Sometimes my friend is mean to me.
Friends like the same things.	My friend likes some things that I don't (for example, carrots).
Friends play with each other.	I don't play with all my friends all the time.
Friends are funny.	Sometimes my friends are sad, and when they are, they are not funny.

Create challenge using some of these questions:

- What is a friend?
- What does a friend look like?
- What does a friend sound like?
- What do friends do?
- What do friends *not* do?
- How do you know if someone is your friend?
- Is it good to have lots of friends?
- Can you ever have too many friends?
- Do you always have to be nice to your friends?
- Are some people better at being friends than others?
- What makes someone a good friend?
- Is a good friend the same as a 'best friend'?
- If a friend won't share his toys, does that mean he is no longer your friend?
- Can you be friends with animals?

- Can you be friends with toys?

- How many different types of friends can you have?

3. CONSTRUCT UNDERSTANDING TOGETHER

Help your children make sense of their thoughts using one or more of the following activities.

Activity 1: Thinking about friendship at home

Ask your children to chat at home with their parents and siblings about friendship. They could find out about the different types of friends their family members may have and then bring in a photograph or a drawing to show friendship.

Questions to help parents help their children:

- What is the difference between being a friend and being friendly?

- How can you tell whether someone (or something) is friendly?

- Is it possible to be friends with a pet or a cuddly toy?

- How is being friends with 'someone' different being friends with something (e.g. with a pet or a cuddly toy)?

Activity 2: Creating the 'perfect' friend

Divide your children into small groups of three or four. Depending on their stage of development, these might be independent groups, or they might be supported by an adult.

Ask one child per group to lie down on a large sheet of paper and get the other children to draw around her to create an outline.

The groups should then work together to create the 'perfect friend' by adding labels and characteristics to the outline. The more creative they can be with the materials available to them, the better. Encourage them to give reasons for each characteristic they give their 'perfect friend' and for the other children to question why those qualities are important.

Ask the children to explain to one another why they think the qualities they are adding to their 'friend' are important. It is essential that each group works collaboratively and builds the 'perfect friend' through meaningful dialogue.

Once their 'friends' are complete, they should present them to all the other children, explaining their thinking. The other groups can question as well as voice support for the ideas.

The following questions could be used as prompts to help your children build their 'perfect' friend:

- Can you build the perfect friend?

- What would they look like?

- How would they behave?

- What would they do?

- What would their interests be?

- Is there such a thing as *one* perfect friend?

Activity 3: Diamond Ranking

After your children have shared their 'perfect friend', you could list/draw/represent the key qualities of a 'friend' that have surfaced from the activity on separate pieces of card. Alternatively, the children can use the resource cards provided in Figure 83.

Introduce the cards to your children, and briefly discuss the meaning of each one. Introduce the idea of the Ranking Frame shown in Figure 64 (page 139), explaining that the best choice is at the top and the worst choice is at the bottom, with OK choices in the middle.

Your children should then work in small groups or as one large group to rank the cards in order of importance. They should place what they feel is the most important feature of a 'friend' at the top and the least important at the bottom, with two cards in the middle showing average importance. Your children should give reasons for their choices and challenges, and counter-examples can be encouraged.

EXTENSION/SIMPLIFICATION

To simplify the activity, the number of cards used could be reduced, or cards could be replaced with photographs or objects to represent the same qualities/statements. The activities could be spread out over several days.

To extend the activity, the Ranking Frame could be increased to a Diamond Nine format so that your children have to place a value on and evaluate more cards in relation to one another at the same time.

4. CONSIDER THE LEARNING JOURNEY

Your children can be given voting cards to respond to the following review statements.

You can use plastic hoops, a box or a large piece of card as an area for the children to cast their votes. Read each statement out, and your children have one vote each per statement. They can vote anonymously or choose to discuss why they have placed their vote where they have. This allows all children to contribute and allows you to get a quick overview of the feelings and attitudes across the group.

Figure 83: Voting cards

Here are some statements to be voted on:

- I understand what it means to be a friend.
- We can all be good friends.
- A friend is always kind.
- You can have many different friends at the same time.
- A friend has to like the same things or have the same interests as you.
- There is no such thing as a perfect friend.
- Friends are very important.

Transfer activities

- Your children can become 'Friendship Detectives' and record or photograph examples of friendship they observe over the course of a day or a week.
- You could share a number of picture books with your children that focus on the concept of friendship such as:

Night Monkey, Day Monkey, Julia Donaldson and Axel Schefler

    The Bear and the Piano, David Litchfield

    The Rainbow Fish, Marcus Pfister

    Pumpkin Soup, Helen Cooper

    Sharing a Shell, Julia Donaldson

- Your children could create some Friendship Rules for their group. (See Figure 84.)

Figure 84: Activity Cards: 'Being a good friend'

Challenging LEARNING 8. Early learning activities Activity 8: Being a good friend

APPENDIX: CODED TRANSCRIPT RELATING TO SECTION 3.6

This is how we would have coded the transcript of the dialogue shown in Section 3.6:

Thomas:	I have got three guinea pigs, a dog and a cat.
Marianne:	That's a lot of pets. (Reflecting)
Ben:	Thomas must really like animals. (Extending)
Helen:	I wonder if he likes all animals. (Extending)
Teacher:	That is a great question, Helen. Before we go any further, can we ask Thomas if Ben was right to say that 'he must really like animals'?
Thomas:	Yes I do.
Helen:	But do you like all animals? (Extending)
Thomas:	Yes.
Teacher:	Can anyone think of examples of animals that Thomas might not like?
Sarah:	I don't think he likes rats. Or snakes. (Extending)
Lucy:	Or lizards. (Extending)
Teacher:	So, Thomas. Lots of people are trying to guess what you think. Can you tell us which ideas are right?
Thomas:	I've got a pet rat.
Helen:	Ah, so he likes rats then! (Reflecting)
Thomas:	But I don't like snakes.
Elisabeth:	Maybe that's because snakes eat rats. (Extending)
Teacher:	What a clever connection to make, Elisabeth. Thomas, is Elisabeth right?
Thomas:	I don't know. I guess.